Introduction and Guide to
Teaching
Primary Science

Dorothy Diamond

A Chelsea College Project sponsored by the Nuffield
Foundation and the Social Science Research Council

Published for Chelsea College, University of London,
by Macdonald Educational, London and Milwaukee

----Teaching Primary Science----

First published in Great Britain in 1978 by
Macdonald & Co (Publishers) Ltd
Maxwell House
74 Worship Street
London EC2A 2EN

Reprinted 1979, 1980, 1981, 1983

© Chelsea College, University of London, 1978

ISBN 0 356 05082 3

Library of Congress Catalog Card Number
77-82977

Project members
for periods between 1970 and 1975

John Bird
Ed Catherall
Dorothy Diamond
Keith Geary
Don Plimmer
Evaluators
Ted Johnston
Tom Robertson

Editor
Keith Anderson
with the assistance of
Nuffield Foundation Science Teaching Project
Publication Department

Printed in Great Britain by
Butler & Tanner Ltd, Frome and London

Acknowledgements

The author and publishers gratefully acknowledge the help given by:

Staff and pupils of
John Chilton School, Little Ealing Middle School, Ravenor Middle School, Southfield Middle School, all in the London Borough of Ealing. Ex-students of Thomas Huxley College, London, W.3.

Illustration credits
Photographs

By kind permission of W. H. Petty, MA, BSc, County Education Officer, Kent, photographer Mike Williams, pages 10, 61
Ardea Photographs, page 39
L. A. Best, page 66
James Fisher, page 9
Shell Photographic Unit, page 37
Terry Williams, all other photographs

Line drawings by GWA Design Consultants

Cover design by GWA Design Consultants

Preface

The ten books published by Macdonald Educational under the series title Teaching Primary Science come from a project sponsored jointly by the Nuffield Foundation and the Social Science Research Council.

The series has been written specifically for class teachers and students in training. The information and help given in the books is intended precisely for non-science teachers, many of whom have had little help with science work at Infant, First, Junior and Middle School levels.

Today head teachers, parents and the outside world frequently demand that pupils should at least have 'done some science' by the age of 11, 12 or 13. But teachers may understandably be hesitant, since they themselves feel insecure in this field. As several teachers commented at an in-service course. 'When we were at school we never really knew what our physics master was on about.' 'And the boys did all the experiments', said one of the group. These books are meant to help such people, and are based on their experience. They provide simple descriptions of inexpensive child-sized activities through which pupils from five years old upwards can learn to work scientifically.

There is no need for a teacher to know all the answers; the scientific attitude involves finding out, and is not concerned at this level with learning sets of facts, or formulae. Science needs curiosity, care and commonsense. These, rather than test tubes or telescopes, are what make activities scientific, and these can be developed with any age group.

Teachers who are currently thinking about science and education are fast realizing that children need many small practical experiences with materials in their early school years. With a wide variety of such experiences to build on they will be able really to understand the more abstract and complex ideas they are expected to deal with in the secondary school and after.

'Watered down grammar school science' is absolutely wrong for primary school children, but they are capable of doing valuable experimental work much earlier than is often realized. As Constance Kamii says in *Piaget in the Classroom* 'The way in which we arrange the classroom situation for waterplay is an example of how we try to build "readiness" for classification around age 7-8, the concept of specific gravity around age 11-12, and a life-long attitude of research based on curiosity and convictions.'

Each book in the series starts from a non-scientist teacher's possible interest or need. The books in no way constitute a 'syllabus', nor should the topics they cover be regarded as 'the most important'. The areas of experience with which they deal, and the methods described, have been found to work in practice. It is hoped that they will encourage teachers first to use them, and then to develop more of their own.

Contents

Introduction to the series

Science used to be considered 'too difficult' for primary school pupils and, in the way it was then taught, this was only too true. Young children cannot cope with abstract ideas.

The second half of the twentieth century is witnessing an exciting and valuable change in the whole pattern of school science for younger children. Four points in particular stand out as important and helpful, both for the children and their teachers:
1 The conscious intention to set children thinking rather than learning by heart.
2 The change in emphasis from teaching (by teachers) to learning through activities (by pupils).
3 The study of the age stages at which children are able to deal with specific ideas and facts in science.
4 The organized provision of many child-sized experiences and small experiments from which each

child can build up a genuine comprehension of important scientific concepts.

Choose your own starting point

The series Teaching Primary Science has been written to offer support in this field to teachers, probationers and students in training whose initial strengths and interests lie elsewhere.

Below are some suggestions:

Paints and materials   for the art and craft teacher, painter, printer, designer;
Fibres and fabrics   for the craft or home economics teacher, needleworker, or weaver;
Candles   for the artist, historian, educationalist, experimenter;
Science from wood   for the D.I.Y. type, toymaker, handicraft teacher, sailor;
Seeds and seedlings   for the infant-teacher, botanist, smallholder. environmentalist;
Musical instruments   for the craftworker, concertgoer, tape-recordist, historian;
Science from water play   for the parent, infant-teacher, Piaget expert and 'mopper-up' of puddles;
Mirrors and magnifiers   for the designer, maths teacher, naturalist, puzzlesolver;
Aerial models   for the paper folder, modelmaker, kite flyer, airpilot, classroom organizer.

Each book starts by using familiar and easily obtainable materials, and leads to scientific experiences which the children can understand and enjoy. Children are far more capable of 'doing' than we often give them credit for, though in the past we have usually offered them abstract concepts long before they were ready. But practical activities lead to beneficial experiences. If we provide them with sufficient related experiences, by offering each time a slightly different angle on the same concept, we may be delighted to find children discovering generalizations for themselves. The children are then able to sum up their own discoveries about things and what they do. This usually takes the form of the 'Ah-ha, now I see what happens' phenomenon. Or in other words, the world makes sense—which is a discovery for life.

Activities and attitudes

Teaching Primary Science is concerned with the sound organization of activities as well as materials. The books contain helpful ideas about starting points, about children's recording and vocabulary, about the use of workcards, and about connections linking science with other parts of school work. In general, science is not isolated from everyday things—and one of the key questions must always be whether the topic is seen by children as relevant to their lives. Facts learnt at this stage, however useful, are much less important than activities and attitudes. Will the children be interested? Will they be able to understand? Can they be given enough experiences to build up basic concepts for themselves? Will they want to go on? Will the activities and our backing help them to think and act scientifically? Being scientific is not a matter of knowing a mass of facts; it is a way of thinking and acting which anyone can practise. Being scientific involves observing carefully, thinking about what one observes, making sensible guesses based on observations, testing these guesses to see if they work, changing the guesses if they don't work, and in general trying to think logically. These steps need to be taken consciously, but are not necessarily difficult. Children of any age can begin on these lines, and an early start will prove to be an enormous advantage later, as will the skills which they learn along the way.

Introduction to the guide

This introductory book consists of chapters which show the teacher how to find the right kind of science in the interests of children. Some sections deal specifically with points of method, resources etc, and show teachers how to choose topics from other books in the series.

Topics of this book

Most of the chapters deal with one type of material of basic interest to children—the kind of thing they bring into the classroom of their own accord. Each subject is looked at in a practical way to see what scientific experiences may be gained from it; what skills—scientific or technical—it enables the children to practise and at the same time enjoy; and what material the teacher can fairly easily have at hand to extend the activity on the basis of the children's own contributions.

What do children like doing most?
What do they do if given a choice?
What objects, ideas and questions do they bring in with them?
Which of these can most profitably be used for scientific activities such as observing, testing, thinking, learning?
What science can we expect children to derive from using the things and ideas they bring?
How can we the teachers best stimulate, encourage, direct, and enjoy their activities with the children?

Children's choice

Children, of any age, given the choice, tend to take most notice of things (whether subjects or ideas) when they fall into definite categories. These may be things which belong to them personally, or things involving action—things which move or react.

The Science Museum in London demonstrates the popularity of 'press-button' exhibits; the favourite pets are those which come when called, purr when stroked, or in some way respond to the child's actions. For example, a guineapig sustains interest because it is a lively animal with a big appetite. A goldfish is of little interest because it is too quiet and inactive.

'The first child said: "What shall we do with these stones?" The second replied: "Oh, you can't do anything with stones. They don't do anything."' (quoted from *Children learning through scientific interests*.) And this, if the stones are in fact worth studying, is where the teacher can use the other category, the personal element, by suggesting to the children that they make a special collection. The stones might be of unusual colour, or stones which have a special use such as lining the bottom of the aquarium. The children rather than the object will be active, but at least something will be happening.

What do children bring in with them?

Things   magnets, mirrors, minibeasts.
Activities   model-making, bubble-blowing, shell collecting.
Ideas   (often adult fantasy) 'I'm driving a Ferrari, brrm, brrm.'
Questions   for genuine knowledge or for attention and prestige.
Knowledge and information   about astronomy, Blue Peter topics, dinosaurs.

How can we use what they bring?

First, by knowing what we want them to experience and to gain from working scientifically. We want them to practise observing accurately, to group things logically, to think about why things happen and to test their thinking practically.

Secondly, we can work out for ourselves what sort of materials the children are likely to bring in and whether they are suitable to introduce work of a scientific quality.

Thirdly, and this is important in a purely practical way, we can have materials available, tucked away in a handy box or cupboard, which we can add to the children's own if necessary, so that the activity becomes a rich and solid experience rather than a thin gleam.

1 Science and children's skills in Teaching Primary Science

'For many primary school children most of their science could be described as the development of the use of scientific skills.' (Dr. Brenda Presst, *School Science Review 201*, June 1976.)

Which skills can we usefully encourage our pupils to attempt, to learn and to practise in their primary science? Almost all recent research seems to show that they are not ready for abstractions, but there is so much they can do which will make the abstract work comprehensible and real when they come to it. Let us welcome the chance to give this abstract work concrete foundations; if we do this the children will have advantages which children of earlier generations have never had.

For everyday purposes we can group the skills in a simple way:
1 Mainly physical skills and manipulations.
2 Skills and techniques needing some thought as well as physical action.
3 Individual 'mind skills'.
4 Socially directed skills, physical and intellectual.

Children inside any age group vary so widely in their development that it is often easy to miss the signs that they have not yet gained a particular skill we expect them to have mastered. As adults we sometimes forget that children have to practise skills we take for granted, so we hurry them on to the next stage. On the other hand, young children are often much more capable on the practical side than would appear from their 'paper' grading.

1 Early physical techniques

Science from water play introduces many activities using water, for which young children need to learn specific skills. These include such things as pouring water, using funnels, discovering about volumes of water and capacity of containers, floating things in water and testing things to see if they float or sink. The Piaget problems of understanding conservation of matter and volume are not solved without a great many small related experiences of this kind, but the concepts are gained so much sooner and more fundamentally if the practical groundwork has been done thoroughly and early.

In Teaching Primary Science *Paints and materials* most of the colourful investigations involve properties of water and ways of handling it, whether through mixing or separating colours, using paint drips, spatter painting, leaf printing, or designing wax resist and colour washes.

Other manual skills are involved in soaking and planting seeds, watering and supporting seedlings, measuring and recording growth. All these learning steps and techniques are illustrated in *Seeds and seedlings*. The simple science in *Musical instruments* introduces many

small skills connected with making and listening to sounds, and with tuning notes and trying ways of changing them. In *Aerial models* there is a great deal of small scale physical, mainly manual, activity in the folding and testing of paper planes and in the production of paper windmills, spinners and kites. Through these activities children gain both new achievements and a basis for understanding.

2 Combined physical and mental skills

These make up a large part of school science in any age group. Observing and thinking about what you observe is stressed in Teaching Primary Science *Candles* and in *Mirrors and magnifiers*. In each book the observations

lead to explanations at different levels, according to the age and experience of the children working them out. Some of the pupils' observations in *Science from wood*, on the other hand, lead rather to thinking about suggestions for practical uses of wood, and the comparison of wood with other materials for similar purposes.

Solving problems   Thinking out and then trying ways to solve problems is a sequence so basic to scientific method that it is found in every book of the Teaching Primary Science series. *Fibres and fabrics* suggests that children should collect samples of fabric scraps and then make their own sorting schemes. Later, known tests are described for identification. Pupils working on *Aerial models* test different variables as they try to make the most efficient paper glider or the most effective spinner or kite.

Safety   Coordinated action and thought are particularly important for safety during practical work. Ways of helping children to see and avoid dangers are suggested, for example in connection with splinters and the use of tools, in *Science from wood*, in the context of the (small) fire risks in *Candles* and *Fibres and fabrics*, and in other details in *Musical instruments* and *Mirrors and magnifiers*. There should be very little need for anxiety in any of these fields.

Economy   Thought and action together are needed in the economical use of materials and resources. If each pupil is to have his or her chance of experimenting, cheap raw materials must be organized. The children can involve themselves in both thinking and acting (see *Aerial models. Science from wood, Seeds and seedlings* and *Musical instruments*). Equally, children need to act thoughtfully in putting away the more expensive or rare materials they have used, especially such things as mirrors or woodwork tools; suggestions are to be found in the relevant books.

3   Individual 'mind skills'

These are what we hope our pupils will learn, develop, practise and enjoy. They are the achievements teachers and writers seem to value most highly. They may include skills such as accurate observation (see *Candles* and

Seeds and seedlings), looking for causes behind effects, making scientific guesses and testing them, asking questions—of people, of books, of the materials, and of themselves (see *Science from wood*). An important 'mind skill' which depends on and grows with the child's experiences as well as his development is that of distinguishing between things, qualities or phenomena. Pupils need to see, handle, feel, measure and hear not just one example of each kind of material but as many examples as possible in order to be able to distinguish with certainty between high and low notes, maize-type and mustard-type seedlings, 'heavy' and 'light' materials, water and other liquids, growth and development in plants. Such skills, based on concrete experiences,

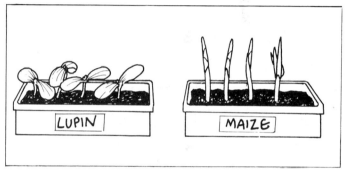

(and all discussed in the TPS texts) lead towards true comprehension of the things around us.

4   Social 'mind skills'

The emotional factors behind social relations in the classroom make this group of skills less susceptible to organization than the others, but at the same time even more important in children's development. Some are simple, such as communication—in words, pictures, models, charts or collages. Others may need considerable guidance from the teacher, though the final product of active work on a scientific topic is often remarkably good simply because it has been based on the children's concrete experiences to which they can all relate.

Discussion of observations or results after an activity in which all have taken part can be so productive that it widens everybody's horizon; if the enthusiasm is there it then leads to cooperation in planning the attack on the next shared problem. In any case talking is vital, either in small groups or as a class. Maybe the kind of discussion which helps most, after one section of activity has been dealt with, is on what to do next, how to do it, what might happen, and why it might happen. The teacher consciously resists the temptation to give the answers before the pupils have had a chance to find out, but steers the discussion by questions and hints on possible methods, supplying new vocabulary (with paraphrase so that everyone understands) as it becomes necessary. Good discussion results in new outlooks and sparks off inventions. Sharing experiences with a group helps the individual in the long process of learning to cope. Discussion can be a constructive scientific activity in its own right.

Bibliography from Teaching Primary Science

Discussion: *Aerial models* p. 35; *Fibres and fabrics* pp. 6, 8, 23-24; *Seeds and seedlings* pp. 13, 19.
Vocabulary: *Paints and materials* pp. 20-22; *Science from water play* pp. 23, 25; *Aerial models* pp. 35-37; *Fibres and fabrics* pp. 4, 5, 13; *Seeds and seedlings* Chap. 8; *Musical instruments* Chap. 7.

Tuning the guitar

2 Balloons, balls and bubbles

This is a trio of related topics which must appeal to every child, and to almost every adult. There are many scientific points to pick up, both of method and of fact, along with the fun. Keep a look-out all the time for things to observe, ideas coming out of observations, logical guesses to be made about events and reasons, ways to test the guesses, and an understanding of what happens.

Balloons first

Start with a packet of round balloons. Try to have one balloon per child if possible, for emotional as well as hygienic reasons—and of course a few spares. The wire-in-paper strip closures for plastic bags make an effective method of securing the neck: twist round once, fold the neck down, twist closure round the doubled-over tube.

Small rubber bands wound around the neck several times also work well. Knots are too difficult to undo, and string is too difficult to tie.

Blowing up balloons the first time is very hard for small children, and as one shouldn't give them one's own germs, the answer is a simple pump—perhaps a cardboard one from a toyshop, or a plastic and metal air-pump from E. J. Arnold, or a borrowed football or bicycle pump. Blow up the balloons half-way the first time, so that the children can experience the stretchy soft texture of the rubber, and the 'squashability' of the air inside.

Workcards to help with organization

Balloons are so closely connected with parties and fairs, and excitement, that a little planned organization is a help in the classroom. Workcards, carefully worded and not too long, provide a steadying framework. They allow for variety, cut out waiting, and can give every pair of pupils something meaningful to do all the time. They can be worded so as to lead to discovery without leaving the children floundering, not knowing what to do next or how to do it.

Several books in the Teaching Primary Science series offer workcard ideas and specimen texts. Here are some more, on the subject of balloons:

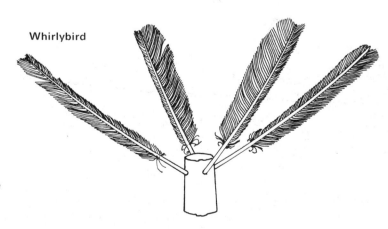

Whirlybird

Get a cork, 4 feathers and a nail

Make 4 slanting holes into the cork and push the feathers in gently

Get all the feathers twisted the same way

Throw the Whirlybird up and watch it drop

Workcards 1 : bouncing balloons

1 Blow up a balloon about half-full of air. Then just let it drop from the edge of the table onto the floor. Notice how far it bounces up again. Do this two or three times to make sure. Mark, or measure, how high it bounces up.

2 Now blow more air into the same balloon, but not enough to burst it. Guess how it will bounce this time— as high as before, higher, or lower? Test your guess as you did before by dropping the balloon off the table top and watching it bounce. What happens this time? Try it twice more to make sure. Does it do what you guessed it would? How can you make a record of what you thought and what you discovered? Can you draw it? Or write down what happened?

Class discussion after experiments like these is very valuable, because so many side-issues evolve spontaneously, such as the difference between the bounce of a sad football with a slow puncture, or a neglected tyre, compared with the bounce of each when fully pumped up. Children with different kinds of background have an opportunity to offer special knowledge, and to build up their own confidence and the interest of the class.

Workcard 2 : air is compressed into a balloon

1 Take your own balloon (avoid anyone else's germs). Blow it up about halfway, pinch the neck, turn the mouth of the balloon to your cheek or your neck, and let the air out. Why does it come out with a rush?

2 Make and hang up a short tissue paper streamer, or make a small paper windmill (if you can make one which turns very easily). Blow up your balloon until it is well stretched, pinch the neck, then let the air out to make it blow the streamer or turn the windmill. You may have to try more than once to get the angle right.

3 Stand a short thick candle or a nightlight safely on a saucer and light it. Blow up your balloon again, and try to make air from it blow out your candle. Keep the rubber away from the flame as you will need the balloon again.

4 Blow up your balloon once more and pinch the neck. Get hold of the sides of the balloon neck with both of your first fingers and thumbs, and pull gently so that the neck of the balloon is stretched flat across. Now slacken your pull a little, so that a little air gets out. What do you notice? Keep on pulling a little more and a little less; what can you make the air from the balloon do?

Some children will be interested to know that this is how our voice boxes work when we sing or speak. The air coming up from our lungs makes the vocal cords vibrate in just the same way as the air from the balloon makes the stretched rubber vibrate. Changes in pitch are due to tightening or loosening the vocal cords (or the balloon rubber).

Workcard 3 : balloons and 'lightness'

1 Balance a balloon over the tip of your finger before you blow it up. Can you feel the weight of the balloon? What are you really feeling the weight of?

2 Blow up the balloon, fasten the neck, and keep the balloon up in the air by giving it little pushes with the same finger. How hard do you have to push? What are you holding up in the air this time?

3 Try to balance the blown-up balloon on the tip of your finger, and feel the weight. The balloon is very much bigger than it was when you felt the weight before; does it feel much heavier? What does this tell you about the weight of air?

Workcard 4 : balloons and water

1 Put some water in a plastic bowl or the sink. Blow up a balloon, fasten the neck, and put it carefully onto the water. Look at the way it floats; look from the top and from the side, and perhaps draw the side view.

2 Push the balloon lower into the water, and feel what you have to do to make it go under. This is used at the swimming baths and the seaside. Make a list of the things you know which use the same idea.

3 Start with a dry balloon, put it on water, and see how much (or how little) of the rubber gets wet. This shows how much of the balloon went under water.

4 Blow up a balloon, hold the neck, and put the mouth of the balloon under water. Then let go *a little at a time.*

5 Sink an opened tin can in the water so that it is full of water. Now blow up a balloon, pinch the neck, hold the neck under water, and see if you can get enough air from the balloon to go into the can to make it float. This is how they raise wrecks from the sea (though of course they don't use air from balloons).

Class discussion   Pull all the discoveries and ideas together, so that a coherent pattern can be found even if some children have not done some of the experiments. The lightness and the 'squashability' of air will have been the two major 'facts' involved, but for many of the pupils the most important will be the lightness of big things if they are filled with air.

The everyday examples the children can think of once they get the idea are considerable: lifejackets, swimming lesson armbands, air-filled rings, canoes, even catamarans. They can find highly coloured illustrations in the travel agents' brochures to start a workbook or project folder.

Ball game balls

Start with a collage of ball games—a rugby player clutching an oval ball, a girl hitting a tennis ball, 7-foot high Americans scoring basketball goals etc.

Measuring   Follow up fast with a collection of games balls from school and home. Children easily learn how to measure diameters of rounded objects using blocks and a ruler, or sliding calipers of the Osmiroid type or made at school from card (see *Seeds and seedlings* pp. 7-8). Draw or cut out circles, and one oval, to show exact ball sizes. Add some circles to show how big a basketball net or golfhole is, to go with the idea that the ball will go in. The circumference of the ball is often stated in the rulebooks. It is simple enough to measure the bigger balls with a tape measure. The complicating factor is likely to be the confusion in rulebooks over inches and centimetres. Providing the school's maths programme permits, it is easiest to measure in both units. Make a graded row of all sizes found, keeping to one unit (cm). Conveniently, football, netball, basketball and water-polo balls are all approximately of the same size, 68 to 71 cm round. Correct ball sizes can be found in

---

Ways of measuring the size of a seed.

1. With your partner collect two wooden blocks, a large seed (coconut, avocado 'stone' or horsechestnut) and a ruler marked in centimetres.

2. Put the blocks on a straight line and a little way apart.

3. Put the seed between the blocks so that each end of it touches a block.

4. Put the ruler along your side of the blocks, with the zero (0 cm) end touching the inner corner of the left hand block on your side.

5. Check with this diagram:

6. Measure the length of your seed.

7. Write down your result.

8. Measure another seed in the same way.

Official Rules of Sports and Games, published by Kaye and Ward; ask in the reference section of the local library.

Weighing   Now what about weighing all available balls? And just out of interest, try a clean dry football, and then the same ball after a wet, muddy game; the rules say 'not less than 14 oz and not more than 16 oz at the start of the game'. Footballers have to be tough.

The weight of a ball tells you more than the size did, for example, will the ball float in water or not? The weight makes a scientific guess possible, so guess first and then test—with a table tennis ball, a large marble, a tennis ball, a golf ball and a plastic football. Young children

1 Testing bounce

a. Find the height of bounce when ball is dropped from a standard height (this is used in the specifications for match tennis balls).

b. Find the angle of bounce—the direction in which a ball will bounce and its connection with the angle at which it is thrown (this is very important for later understanding of reflection of light in physics). The actual testing can best be done by rolling a ball at an angle to a smooth wall and watching how it bounces away from the wall. Rolling has two advantages over the usual vertical bouncing—the ball doesn't hit windows, and it is easy to mark the angles on the floor with chalk.

often think big things must sink and little things float, this material will help them to find out for themselves.

Maths   Grouping into (mathematical) sets follows very easily: floating or sinking, hollow or solid. A third possible grouping, though not quite so clearly defined, is 'good bouncers' and the 'bad bouncers'. This is well worthwhile because of its similarity to the hollow/solid set. If children make collages of the two groupings the similarity soon shows, and some of them will be able to add ideas from more adult sports, such as billiards, played with heavy solid balls whose 'bounce' comes only from the edges of the billiard table. What about bowls and ten-pin bowling bowls, and pin-ball balls and the small soft dark green squash balls? There is so much opportunity for simple scientific experience and thinking here that a keen group of children could go on working on it for weeks.

Vocabulary   Vocabulary work is involved from the beginning; for example, we all say a football is round, but we all know it should be a sphere. Young children have to find out the difference between solid and hollow, and what there is inside a hollow object. This is easy if there is a split tennis ball around when they are testing 'floating or sinking', because they can float it and then fill it with water to see what happens. With luck and a little help they will actually see the air coming out of the split as the water goes in and the ball gets heavier.

Extensions   Here are three suggestions from amongst the many possible extensions:

2 Rolling a small ball   Roll a marble, golf ball or table tennis ball down a slope onto a flat surface and measure the distance it rolls along the flat. This gives some very good starting experiences for the study of slopes and gradients, and much later of acceleration. Besides which, it is fun. The children working-playing at it need not know that they are using the same method as Galileo used, but if they find that the steeper the slope of their runway the further the ball goes on rolling along the floor, they have grasped a fundamental principle for good. (See *Science from wood* p. 19.)

3 History, science and technology   often meet; balls for throwing and kicking have been around for literally thousands of years, but it is only in about the last hundred years that balls have really bounced since they began to be made of rubber. Before then many different fillings were tried. Older juniors could make and test all sorts of materials: sawdust, crumbled spongy plastic, hay (used in Elizabethan times) in small plastic bags, woolly balls as on bobble caps. The criteria could be that the ball is suitable for throwing and catching or hand tennis, and does not hurt bystanders or break windows. The Chinese tissue paper and string ball is good for fine weather. A spherical case of felt or fabric is not too easy to construct, but a nylon stocking can be tied into a ball shape. The panels in football covers and tennis balls show how difficult it is to make this shape. Children can however produce satisfactory, though fragile, spheres by pasting strips of tissue paper over an ordinary blown-up balloon, allowing it to dry, and then letting the air out so that the balloon can be rescued. If the globe is not needed as a lantern it can be cut up like orange peel from South Pole to North Pole, and spread out to form Mercator's Projection found in every atlas. (See Ladybird *Understanding Maps* pp. 8-9.)

Bubbles

Starting   Whatever the age group, bubble-blowing is bound to make a bit of a wet mess. Newspapers will absorb a lot of it, and an old hand towel is invaluable (not school paper towels as they are more useful for damp-cleaning). Workcards need to be protected by some kind of waterproof plastic covers.

Put the bubble mixture into several coffee jar lids and hand these out amongst the class. This makes sure the children reach the liquid easily. Also have a few old saucers available for experiments. Tall jars and pots are too liable to get knocked over. You can of course buy bubble mixture, but washing-up liquid diluted with water works well; try $\frac{1}{4}$ 'Fairy' to $\frac{3}{4}$ water. The teacher needs to try out a quick bubble or two beforehand, since the best proportions for good results vary with brands of liquid. Each pupil needs a straw, a plastic one rather than waxed paper as these go soggy when used. Some wire, of the kind telephone engineers pull out of their cables, or of similar thickness, a small plastic funnel, and a jam or coffee jar will increase opportunities for both testing and thinking.

Workcard 1

1 Blow a few bubbles into the air, using a straw dipped into the bubble mixture or diluted washing-up liquid. Notice the shape of each bubble carefully—the single bubbles, the twins and the triplets. What shape are they when they are not touching anything (except air), and what happens to the shape where two are joined together? Look at several pairs and triplets to make sure.

2 Wet a flat plate or saucer with bubble liquid. Blow a bubble and let it land on this wet surface. What happens to the shape of your bubble? Draw this shape.

3 Dip the end of your straw in the bubble mixture and blow some bubbles on to the saucer. Try to make just a few big bubbles which will cover the saucer between them. Look down on top of the bubbles; what happens to the shape where they touch?

4 Take a clean milk bottle or glass jar. Put a little washing-up liquid and water in the jar, put your hand over the top, and shake carefully until you have some big bubbles in the jar. If you look very carefully you can count the sides of one or two of the bubbles in the middle. How many are there? Can you make the same shape from a lump of Plasticine remembering how many sides the bubbles had?

Workcard 2

1 Take a plastic funnel and some bubble mixture. Try to make a bubble by dipping the wide top of the funnel into the liquid, lifting it out, and then blowing through the

narrow end of the funnel. You may have to try several times. Can you shake the bubble off the funnel? Can you see any way to make a bubble using the narrow bottom end of the funnel?

2 Take a piece of wire and bend one end into a circle. Then dip the circle into the bubble mixture, hold it up in front of your mouth, and blow gently into the middle of the film across the ring of wire. Try this several times; the wire may not have a film across the ring every time. When you do it next time, watch the shape of the film while you are blowing (this is not too easy). Blow very gently, then harder, then harder still. Do you see how the force of your blowing stretches the film? What does the film do (before it breaks) if you blow just a little and then stop blowing? Can you blow a stream of bubbles from your wire ring? If you have a pot of shop bubble mixture there may be a plastic ring on a handle inside, try with this.

3 Bubbles do not usually last a long time. Here is a way to try and make a bubble last longer. Take a fairly big glass jar such as a coffee jar, a saucer, a wire or plastic ring and some bubble mixture. Attach some Plasticine to the foot of the wire loop or plastic ring so it can stand up in the saucer. Now make the saucer and jar wet inside, blow a bubble and catch it on the ring, stand the ring on the saucer, and quickly turn the wet jar upside down over it. Then watch, you may be lucky enough to keep your bubble for half an hour. You will also be able to see the colours changing slowly while you wait. Can you think why a bubble inside a wet jar can last longer than one out in the open? What is different for the bubble in the jar? What do you think makes the one out in the open burst? The bubble dries up, of course. But keeping it in a moist atmosphere helps—and children always want a bubble to last.

Discussion   What do we want children to get out of such activities? Class discussion can give us a good idea of what they have already gained, and it will enable us to guide the talk in the way they benefit most from it. Some general ideas will emerge if we ask for them. As a summary, we can say that balloons, balls and bubbles have many things in common: they are mostly air-filled, mostly spherical, mostly able to bounce, and most have a springy skin or case. Extensions to this cover a very wide field.

But other gains may perhaps be even more important:

Enjoyment in experimenting and observing.
Satisfaction from measuring, comparing and relating things with one another.
Making scientific guesses based on practical experiences and testing these guesses.
Trying to think out reasons and explanations.

Throughout they will have been cooperating, communicating and extending their awareness of a scientific background to familiar things in the twentieth century world.

3 Brighter teaching, and learning, by overhead projector

The overhead projector is a superb classroom aid in the teaching of science, but often sadly under-used. How else *can* you show a class, or even a group, the eight hairy legs of Jenny's dead spider, or the precision with which two small cog wheels mesh together in Petra's old alarm clock? And with an overhead projector it is so easy, and so memorable. Many Junior and Middle Schools have an overhead projector, and some Infant and First schools too. The screen can be very cheap—a patch of white wall or a square of matt white hardboard. The best position for this screen is hung across the front corner of the classroom next to the window, tilting slightly forward at the top.

The transparent 'acetate' plastic squares to write or draw on (from E. J. Arnold or Ofrex, for example) are not very expensive, and can be used time and time again with the correct pens (eg Staedtler Lumocolor, water-based). The acetate sheet is simply wiped clean with a damped soft tissue or kitchen towel; keep a roll and a squeezy bottle of water handy. School paper towels make smudges, they are meant for tougher jobs.

Using spirit-based Lumocolor Permanent pens one can make 'everlasting' transparencies for material one needs to repeat. This means an enormous saving in time and effort, with no 'cleaning off' or 'taking down and putting up'. Save your energy for essentials.

What are the main advantages of using an overhead projector?

1 The image of the picture, text or object is very large, bright, and clear, and can be seen by a whole class at the same time. It can be changed or moved instantly, and is completely under the control of one person, teacher or pupil, at the working surface of the projector. This person is also, of course, facing the class and can at once respond to their suggestions, or ask them for ideas or answers.

The colour is normally brilliant unless solid objects are being shown, and if the screen is in the right place, there is no need for window blinds. The brightness and colour are stimulating.

2 Several methods of using it are available to the teacher, for example:
(i) You can build up a picture, diagram or 'story-line' by adding overlays, starting with a bare outline and adding matched sheets of acetate each carrying more detail or colour etc.
(ii) A second ploy is to begin with a complex picture (perhaps of an object as it normally appears) and then to take off layer by layer the external or complicating material until the basic 'skeleton' is left. One or more of the overlays used may be opaque (just paper) so that an important part of the text or image is not seen until a late stage. This stimulates the formation of hypotheses.

Adding material bit by bit can be done on the spot by hand, as on the old blackboard, but removing layer after layer of a drawing or object is only for overhead projectionists.

3 A transparent sheet ruled in centimetre squares can be laid on the horizontal glass 'table' of the projector, and used to show the size of the object being projected, since it is magnified equally. It can be turned into a bright, easily seen bar chart to demonstrate the results of an investigation, or it can serve as a very clear example of magnification, eg for the study of the scale of a plan, map or diagram. The centimetre-squared grid is excellent for use in finding the area of irregular flat shapes, such as leaves, since you can see the outline being drawn on the grid, the squares and parts of squares being counted; the class or group can all take part in helping the individuals on the job. The grid can be washed

afterwards, and nothing is wasted or even used up. Acetate sheets on the overhead projector, plain or grid, make one of the best possible methods of communicating directly between the individual and the group, and results which are worth keeping or are needed again, can be kept as long as required.

Children and the overhead projector

Projectors are usually thought of as the teacher's prerogative, therefore the opportunity for pupils to practise on the projector is highly prized; the Hawthorne effect—the motivation due to 'special treatment'—can be used to the full. The overhead projector is not particularly vulnerable, so there is no need to keep an anxious hold on it.

It has many great advantages: children can work singly or in small groups when making and showing transparencies, their material can be altered and improved in seconds, and the 'competence motive' leads to considerable effort and to personal satisfaction. The least confident children can take their time over 'getting it right' before showing a transparency, and those who most need help can trace starter outlines or plan on paper in pencil and trace when ready. The slow worker is able to present to the class in a moment a drawing or idea which may have taken hours to prepare; the ease of alteration gives the less-confident child the feeling that it is always possible to improve and improve.

Making transparencies for overhead projectors is an exceptional activity for children. A set of transparencies can be an immediate objective for group work, which the whole class can then see and discuss together. Satisfactory products can be filed easily; children's own ideas, experiments, inventions, guessing games, classification groupings, identification keys, discoveries traced from books, all become available in a way which would be impossible on paper. And on the teacher's side, a lively transparency makes a fine focus of attention and observation, say in the last five minutes of the day.

4 Making things and seeing the science

What have you found your pupils really like making? Things with funny faces on them? Try simple origami, or mobiles, or kites. What about things they can compete with? Try paper gliders or a roll-ball alley. How about things meant to surprise you: maybe a little bob-up man or an impossible-looking poodle standing on its hindlegs? Or perhaps brightly-coloured circles of pattern — then try a simple kaleidoscope.

In the Teaching Primary Science series we suggest a good many things children can do to help their learning of science and to practise scientific methods. In this chapter we look at things which pupils do for fun, and see what science materializes.

Choice of topic

It is obviously impossible to have each child doing his or her own thing: we would so often come up against the conflicting interests of the bright as compared with the less able child, or against the traditional (and probably also biological) gap between boys' and girls' activities. However, the teacher can judge and nudge to get things going.

Marble games

Most children enjoy these, though their reasons may differ; it would be interesting to try to identify them.

1 The two boys in the photograph (from *Science from wood*) with their roll-ball alley investigated, first by accident and then by intention, the effect of the slope of the runway on the distance the marbles would roll along

A child's drawings of 'half-people'

A child's drawings of 'half-faces'

A roll-ball alley

the floor. They could also have tested the result of running the marbles onto lino, as in the photograph, onto a thin smooth layer of sand or a flat sheet of glass-paper, or onto carpet tiles, all from the same position of their runway. However, this would have been a completely different experiment, testing the effects of friction on the marble glass. It was not suggested to them, because they needed to grasp one major new idea clearly before another was introduced.

2 A number of glass marbles under a tin lid gives a pleasing feeling of free movement on a smooth table top. With a load of books balanced on the tin lid the ball-bearing effect is most convincing, especially when compared with what happens if one attempts to pull the load without the marbles. Even more like real engineering is a glass marble ball-race, again showing the reduction in friction due to smooth glass and the very small surface of a sphere touching a flat table top. For the ball-race one needs three tin lids chosen for size: one small, one medium and one large. The smallest lid goes edge-downwards in the middle of the next, which is edge-upwards; a ring of marbles goes between these. The largest lid caps the collection, and a load on top of it spins round in a convincing way when gently pushed. Here is one of the many ways in which science and

engineering meet, and for children this is always important, since it shows scientific ideas as part of everyday life, and not just something people do in laboratories.

3 Making a marble maze   An expanded polystyrene ceiling tile, some strips cut from a second tile (or just bits), some pins (to be replaced by Copydex when the maze has been tested), and a glass marble make a good maze; its construction needs thought. The extension activity is to use a fairly large steel ball-bearing instead of the marble, and to control it by using a magnet hidden under the tile. This is a nice piece of science; to get the marble where you want it, you have to tilt the maze this way and that, often unsuccessfully. The ball-bearing can be steered exactly on a horizontal maze without any problem. Car repair workshops may well have odd ball-bearings to spare.

Making things stand up firmly

Many things in the classroom, models of people, trees, castles . . ., are there waiting to be cut out, on paper, card or even plywood, but the problem has always been to make them stand up. In fact, they have often proved disastrously disappointing, leaning unhappily or collapsing when the door opens, or sliding onto the floor. Several books on model-building have now produced very good ideas to improve the stability of card structures. The principle to use is the one which holds the partitions in boxes for 12 bottles of wine—the 'two-slots' method. The simplest example is to use a wine box, which children can study as an introduction. There is no need to tell them how to do it when they can take the partitions to pieces and put them together again several times until the principle is completely clear. A slot from the bottom to halfway up the middle of a cut-out owl fits exactly into a similar slot from the top to halfway down the middle in the second cut-out. The standing owl on the shelf in the photograph was made by a pupil, using a junior hacksaw and a nail file, from the side of a greengrocers' fruit tray.

The improvement which allows much more adaptability in standing structures consists simply of making more slots in any one sheet of card or plywood; two slots

The standing owl on the shelf in the photograph below was made by a pupil, who used a junior hacksaw and a nail file, the wood was obtained from the side of a greengrocer's fruit tray, as illustrated above

across will hold a shelf, two down will keep a curved or folded structure in place. Four books can be recommended for this kind of activity which may appeal to both teachers and children.

George Aspden's *One Piece of Card* (Batsford, 1973) gives patterns for rather complex figures, boats and birds. He makes the point that such structures can be immediately dismantled, and packed flat. He urges that the scissors used for card should be sharp enough to cut rather than chew.

Christmas Magic by M. Perry (Mills & Boon, 1965) uses the 'two-or-more slot' method for many decorations include a cat and her kittens, which have proved very popular.

The Know-How Book of Paper Fun by A. Curtis and J. Hindley (Usborne, 1975) produces trees and castle

walls held up by this engineering principle.

Chester Jay Alkema in *Creative Paper Crafts* (Sterling/Oak Tree Press, 1967) in an attractive but very expensive book shows how to put together many of what he calls three dimensional stabiles in this way. (NB the dictionary gives stabiles (stay-biles) as a partner to mobiles.)

Science and standing up

Children can try a large number of small tests to find out what gives structures, such as their model buildings, animals and trees, the capacity to stand up firmly without guy-ropes or roots. This is the kind of exercise which can stretch the really bright—and inventiveness needs practice.

They all know that models will not stand up on one leg, and that they are pretty unstable on two; but with a back strut as many card models have, the three-legged object is stable. A lump of Plasticine and a few glass-headed pins provide good material for testing these ideas. What about a one-pin stalked toadstool? No, of course not, it wouldn't work. A two-pin legged bird? Equally not. A three-legged stool? Or a kangaroo of Plasticine with a good solid tail as its 'third leg'? Yes, but wait a minute, suppose the three legs were all in a row? Will this work? No again.

Think of the standing structure of the ordinary things which have no problems: the four legs of a table (or a horse, which can go to sleep on them), or the square base of the telephone, or the circular base of a tube standing up, or the 6, 8, 10 . . . wheels of a locomotive. Or indeed the four wheels of a skateboard. What do we actually need to make an object stand steadily? It seems to be a base which takes up space, doesn't it? Even if you stand a sheet of card or hardboard against the wall, unless it projects a little way at the bottom it will not be safe. Some child ought now to ask; 'What about us? Our feet aren't all that large.' To which the answer, as always, is two more questions: 'What would happen if we tried to go to sleep standing up?' and 'Don't we get tired of standing?' That is, we have to work with our muscles to stay upright; our pins and cardboard models can't do it that way.

But there are all sorts of methods which children can try to give their constructions stability: the zigzag screen form, the triptych folds, etc.

Keeping the weight down

A very bright child might by now have thought of the little bob-up man, with his hemisphere base and almost no contact with the table top at all. Now what about this 'base taking up space'? Well, the bob-up isn't stable, of course, though he does come upright again after being pushed over. But it is in just this that he is particularly interesting.

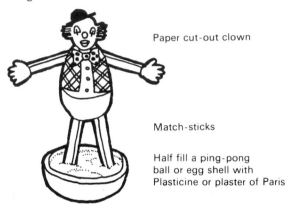

Paper cut-out clown

Match-sticks

Half fill a ping-pong ball or egg shell with Plasticine or plaster of Paris

A pop-up man

Make a few of these models, sometimes called 'wobbly-men', take half of an old table tennis ball. Put a lump of Plasticine inside it, stick a cork into the Plasticine, and make the head by slotting card into the cork or by pinning a small stuffed nylon sphere on to it. Push them over—up they come again. Why? Because all the weight is at the bottom. Now try something which seems to contradict all the pin-leg experiments: the balancing poodle (or pony, or . . .). It needs another cork, five pins (with glass heads if possible), a little bit of fluffy wool, a large safety-pin or a piece of wire, and some kind of weight, say a key. A fluffy head on one pin goes into the cork, a bit of fluff for a tail is stuck or slotted into the other end, it has four pin legs, and the safety-pin is pushed into its tummy, with the key hanging on the clip end of the pin. Balance the animal on its back feet on the tip of your finger; it will rock, but it stands there on two feet. The secret is of course that the greatest weight, and hence the centre of gravity, of the whole thing is below the level of its feet; this can't happen with objects standing on a table or on the floor. So the 'rules' are not quite the same. There are other nice toys working on the same lines as the little cork animal, perching parrots with heavy tails, for example. Children may well find patterns for making them in craftwork books.

Two more books containing very good ideas for making things by folding paper are, Macdonald Starters Science *Folding and Unfolding,* and S. Lewis and L. Oppenheimer's *Folding Paper Puppets* (Muller, 1964). In the models suggested in each of these books the makers will find a great deal to involve them in problems of symmetry, of judgement, of the finer manual skills, and of three-dimensional construction. At the same time they will be discovering inventiveness, and maybe practising it for themselves.

Mobiles

Mobiles, as opposed to stabiles, demand a different aspect of physics: the 'balance' principle. The construction of mobiles, for this reason, is not very easy, and young children become frustrated if the units hang badly askew or come off the ends of the crossbars. The main principle is to start at the bottom, and get one horizontal to balance at a time, working upwards. Some wire coathangers have a downward curve at each end of the bottom wire. This is a help, not only for mobiles but also in using the coathanger as a simple balance with some kind of scale-pans hanging from the ends, such as ice-cream tubs.

Mobiles of fish have a second scientific aspect: the makers may look more carefully at real fish, or at good pictures, in order to make the models realistic. On the other hand, the flying fish can be quite imaginary. Children often learn in making such models the existence and position of fins, gill-covers and types of tail—all of these facts promote their scientific knowledge and help to make the mobile more varied. Good sunfish can easily be constructed from two paper plates, upper sides inwards, and glued or stapled round the edges with the inclusion of appropriate fins and tail.

27

Stapler work is extremely popular with pupils. The stapler gun is however a rather dangerous weapon, and is not recommended.

At Christmas the shops often have long metal foil strips creased into 'spirals' (actually helix is the mathematicians' word). These spin when hung up in a classroom or school hall; the science is pleasing—warm air from people rises, and turns the foil strip as it does so. With a little care and investigation amateur twirlers can be made from kitchen foil. The most important factor is probably the fine thread from which the strip is hung. It needs to be fairly long. Of course, those who know how it works will choose a position over a source of heat, eg the radiator.

Boats and floats

Given adequate water-containers, there are few children who do not enjoy to the full a session making and floating all kinds of model boats.

Books often suggest tests for streamlining, but the difference between a sharp point or a blunt one at the front end of a piece of expanded polystyrene ceiling tile is negligible, since so little of the 'boat' is in the water anyway. Much more interesting is the unsinkability of the stuff, and hence its value to people learning to swim at the local baths.

An excellent small problem for experimenters in the classroom is to think out all the ways of loading an egg-box made from the bottom half of one of those pink, blue or yellow opaque plastics, so that the boat stays level. If the cargo is large glass marbles, several alternative hypotheses can be tried and found successful. The box base can then be cut down the middle with scissors and made into a catamaran with a centre board cut from the box lid. One of the most educational activities using model boats is the discovery by trial, and often error, of the importance of a keel and the relative difficulty of supporting a large sail.

Building boat replicas is a time-consuming activity and for the enthusiast only, especially as most replicas are

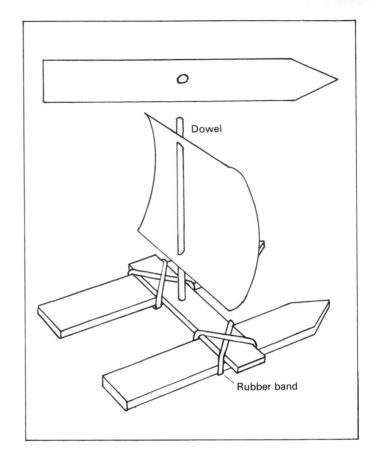

only for show, not for floating. A simple model of something as primitive as the Kon-Tiki is another matter, as the illustration shows. This, however, needs a large water surface to suggest an ocean. In that case a sail should be rigged and winds simulated in a variety of ingenious ways. The back end of a horizontal vacuum-cleaner gives a constant wind-supply that can be used for testing the efficiency of sail designs.

General skills

In the making of models, card structures, mobiles, stabiles, or boats, there are general small skills which children can be encouraged to pick up as they go along. For example, there are good ways of fixing things together, of making holes which will not tear, of

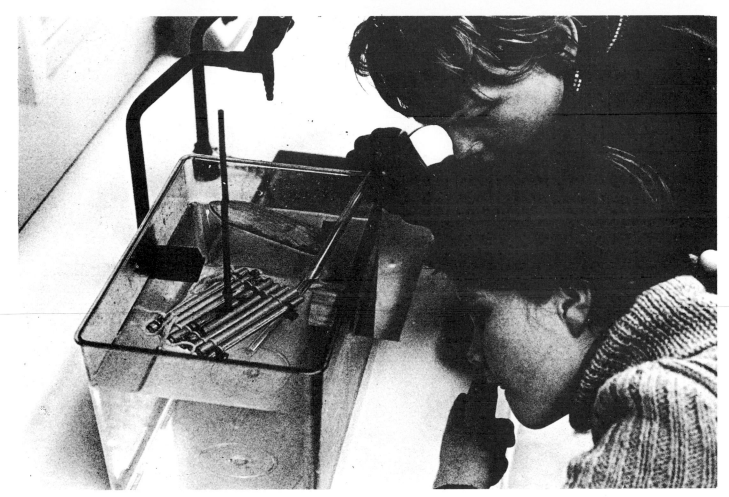

Testing the Kon-Tiki

strengthening weak points, and of avoiding personal harm (eg by remembering that fresh edges of paper can cut skin quite painfully). In addition to the principles which appear as the activities develop, these small skills help children to enjoy what they are doing and to feel confident and competent in practical situations. They will be better able to deal with more advanced science later in their school careers.

What particular small skills would you think most necessary for your own pupils to acquire, if they have not already done so? How do you find that they pick up these most efficiently—by being taught them, or by finding them out as they go along?

5 Classroom plants and animals

Why have animals or plants in the classroom at all? They are, after all, rather a nuisance; they need to be looked after, as if a class wasn't enough . . . Probably the most important reason is that, unlike any other non-human object in the room except the clock, they *do something*. And it is of great satisfaction to a child if anything reacts to what he or she does. If the gerbil actually comes and eats the offered peanut ('my' peanut) or the snail shows a preference for 'my' slice of apple, this is an event which will be reported at home in the evening.

Organization Before hopes are raised, the space has to be found. If there isn't enough space, then do not have live animals in the classroom. The sad cooped-up rabbit or budgerigar in a cage under a side table is not a good educational example for children. And pale weedy-looking peaplants are no advertisement for scientific commonsense either. Wide windowsill or clear well-lighted table—yes; temporary shelving for seed-trays (see *Seeds and seedlings*)—yes; a wall-shelf for an aquarium or snailery—yes, as these do not need too much light. But one of the most basic reasons for thinking about having living things in the classroom is to teach children to be considerate to their small captives—and living space is where it begins.

What shall we keep, assuming space is found? Books by enthusiasts propose all sorts of species. If we go through the list carefully thinking about teaching children to be humane, we have to say a firm no to most of them. Space is one problem, another is that even a class of only 30 has altogether 240 fingers, and the animals must have an area where they can at times escape from the children. A rabbit in a hutch is too large, too soft and too vulnerable. Besides, there is the ever-recurring problem of weekends, half-terms and school holidays. Even a normal weekend adds up to about 66 hours, and there

are other things to be done on Monday mornings.

Two species can be recommended for classroom conditions: gerbils (given good homes for all holidays longer than a long weekend), and snails.

Gerbils are more lively than hamsters in the daytime, they are not afraid of people (put your hand in the cage and they climb on to it), they can live very well on pet-shop pellets (you can give them enough to last for a week without worrying), they drink very little water (and that out of a drinking-bottle which holds enough for a week), and—because of the last point—if they have paper and sawdust on the floor of the cage, they only need cleaning-out weekly, and hardly ever even smell. They reproduce fairly often, it varies from gerbil to gerbil, but they do not mind your looking at their babies, nor do they fight if they have been brought up together. There is one small precaution to take, that is to handle the 'adolescents' watchfully, as they can, and do, jump straight up into the air out of your hand.

Snails are excellent animals to study for even the youngest children, the most important factor of all being the 'built-in handle'. If a mouse or a bird struggles in the hand, the child squeezes harder, and may cause the animal internal damage or crushed ribs. Children may

ventilation holes have to be closed with muslin (cotton bandage) taped on, or the baby snails may go on a walkabout. Science 5/13 *Minibeasts* has suggestions on keeping and observing snails. Lenses (about ×2½) are really needed. They should be hand-lenses so that they can be moved as the animal moves. Experiments with different foods are fine, and one can see the small mouth at work. Observations on movement along a plastic ruler or on the underside of plain clean glass are good. Measurements of speed, and distance crawled, too easily become competitive, and competitive children become insensitive. The snail's skin does not protect it, and even thoughtful children may not know, or may be led to ignore the fact that poking, and things like salt, will 'hurt' the snail. A few will try it deliberately, and will repeat it if adults tolerate this. Some books are far from helpful in this matter, showing children stretching worms to measure them, for example, or soaking the lawn in formaldehyde (which makes our eyes sting badly) just to make all the worms come up out of their holes. This is not education.

The school cat's kittens Two eight-year old girls borrowed these for a lunch-hour. Their overheard conversation shows some points about the development of scientific attitudes:

Jannie: 'Mine's lovely and soft—I'd like to cuddle it all afternoon.'
Beatrice: 'Yes, they're fluffier than their mother. I expect it's cold in school at night.'
Jannie: 'I gave mine some of my biscuit at breaktime, but it didn't seem hungry.'
Beatrice: 'Look at their pointed little teeth when they try to bite your finger. Their mother had a mouse on the lawn yesterday.'
Jannie: 'Horrid thing. Mine's paws feel so soft.'
Beatrice: 'They've got little pink pads underneath—and you can see where the claws tuck in.'
Jannie: '... and mine's got a sweet little face.'
Beatrice: 'Their eyes bulge—and the black bit in the middle is only a slit—the big cat's eyes were huge and round when we went home yesterday.'

At the same chronological age, these two children are at very different stages. Development is not a thing you can teach, but maybe they learn from one another. Observation. such as Beatrice was using, comes very

dislike handling slimy things, but the snail's shell is hard, dry and patterned and just right for holding. Looking a snail in the face, one gets a person-to-person impression; eyes on stalks, tiny mouth underneath, feelers below the eye-stalks, a flexible neck-and-body, and a breathing-hole opening under the edge of the shell—like a swimmer taking a breath while doing the crawl. It will feed most gratifyingly on the slice of apple or carrot the child feeds it (so long as it has harmlessly gone unfed the previous day). At weekends or holidays if it gets dry it simply retreats into its shell, makes a thin 'front door', and goes to sleep until you wake it up by wetting it.

An old plastic aquarium makes the best snailery; all

early to some children; adults often over-ride it because they want or expect a different 'answer'. Living things are so variable—every one different—that children encouraged to observe can all produce their own unique results.

Recording

This can be a problem. Children become engrossed in doing things, and may not be at all interested in recording, they have no time for it and find especially the writing a chore and a hindrance, if not actually a difficulty. How can we persuade them that their own observations, measurements, results, discoveries and ideas are too valuable to be lost? The motivation of 'I was the one who saw it, thought of it'—a taste of achievement—if not too frequent, is strong enough to trigger off drawings or models. Shared information is seen by all if it is put on the overhead projector (see page 22), and this starts off discussion. The overhead projector method is also a great help if any measurements, for example the 'weights' (masses) of gerbil families, are being found. Results can be put on the acetate square for all to see, especially if a table with columns and lines has already been drawn. Such prepared sheets can be made without text in permanent (spirit-based) ink ready for all such class-enterprises. For small animals deep pan balances are the best (eg Invicta Rocker or Osmiroid Beamer). E. J. Arnold and Invicta have good plastic 1-gram masses which can simply be counted into the other pan. A 'spring balance' is of course a nonsense; it has no balancing pattern, and measures a force (gravity). Modern spring scales are

Hatching tadpoles

marked in newtons, which is likely to confuse the child with a gerbil.

Plants in the classroom

Plants are too slow for many children. One can however begin where their interests lie, for example by looking at the structure of the fruits and seeds we call peanuts (see *Seeds and seedlings* p. 25), and by growing some of the gerbils' sunflower seeds in eggboxes of sawdust in a mini greenhouse (p. 11). Then other seeds come to mind: maybe plants such as radishes, which grow fast and can be eaten? Apart from seeds, cuttings of tradescantia, geranium or Busy Lizzie are successful and tolerant for growing in classroom pots. Dipping the cut ends in hormone rooting powder *(keep away from small children)* gives the new plants a good start.

Keeping your seedlings moist

1 half egg box

2 seeds in damp sawdust

3 sticks (lolly sticks?) through holes

4 plastic bag

Classroom aquarium

The aquarium on the shelf rather easily becomes part of the wallpaper. It would be different if fish had fur and squeaked. There are several 'fun' techniques to be learnt, however, as well as learning all about fish and waterweed. Why do we leave the topping-up water to stand overnight instead of just taking it from the tap? (To warm up, and to lose its disinfecting chlorine.) How can we pour it in without stirring up every little thing that lies on the bottom? (Lay a piece of paper on top of the water already there, and pour gently onto the middle of it.) How do we get the mess out of the bottom without leaving the goldfish high and dry? (Use narrow plastic tubing, from Boots' D.I.Y. wine department, as a siphon. But if so, the operator needs lots of practice with clean water first, to avoid a mouthful of sludge.) A large clean plastic syringe is perhaps safer, so long as the person in charge empties it before use in the aquarium. In both cases, siphon or syringe, watchfulness is important— only take out what needs to be taken out.

Tadpoles Do use these, but with real concern for the quality of their life. Frogs are becoming rare in Britain, and mainly because of people. Remember the following points: put them in a large dish, not a jar; follow the same water precautions as for the aquarium (above); feed them on very small scraps of raw meat which you remove after one day; take the froglets back to their home pond as soon as their tails begin to shrink (otherwise they starve to death). Stewart Plastics lunch boxes make first class mini-aquaria for close study of all pond creatures of minibeast size. For a little research sideline, start several miniponds using margarine tubs. Keep the same amount of the same pondwater in each tub. Float one leaf of duckweed in each tub and you will see how it multiplies.

6 Using museums and zoos

What do we do at the zoo?

1 Going to the zoo, that is, actually getting there, needs a certain amount of exact planning and organization.
The following points should be checked with the school authorities:

a. Date—make sure it doesn't clash with other planned school outings or activities.
b. Which pupils, how many, how many staff, which staff; inform other teachers.
c. Inform school dinner service.
d. Transport—by what method, who pays?, cost?, booking, departure time, return time.
e. Information to pupils and parents—what to take: food, clothing, eg comfortable shoes for walking and standing, rainwear in case of wet weather, money for booklets, postcards, drinks. *NB* no food for animals these days.

2 What is the visit for? Advance planning, plan of the zoo, plan of the work—any lecture or tour?

3 What will be needed? Worksheets, paper for drawings and notes, clipboard, pencils, rubbers, biros. Arrange meeting-places and times. Prepare some hints on behaviour.

4 Ideas for follow-up by pupils and by teachers, eg establishing or extending picture library (see p. 64) with postcards; photographs of zoo animals, or pupils, or both together, colour slides for in-school use and/or P.T.A. meeting.

5 Books for reference Before the visit and after it. There are very many Animal Encyclopaedias, but it is a good idea to sort out some information on specific ideas which fit the work planned, eg good Ladybird books on mammals from different geographical areas; illustrated books on tropical fish if the aquarium is a target area; Caroline Medawar's set of Chatto Fours on *Primates* if the evolution of man is to be a main topic. These last—the sets of Chatto Fours—are not only superbly illustrated, but also have maps of the world inside the front covers to place the animals in their setting. After all, the collection of animals from all over the world inside one zoo gives a child an impossible ecological picture.

6 Work in the zoo : what should we do?
a. **Observe** helped by theme suggestions, such as *teeth* (hippo, tiger, crocodile, monkeys) *feet* (elephants, bears, camels, orang) *tails, noses, beaks,* etc.

b. **Look for** eg camouflage patches and stripes (tapirs, snakes, giraffes; 'Miss, which way do the stripes on a zebra go?' Can you answer without looking?).

c. **Find out** answers to specific questions thought of in advance with the class, or 'as much as you can about the animals you have chosen for your special study'. This approach is not only appreciated, but may bring in a remarkable accumulation of detail, especially if a keeper happens to be around at the right time.

d. **Compare or contrast** two different types of bird (eagle and owl), monkey, etc.

e. **Draw sketches** eg of body-shapes in fish, or eyes of twilight and night-creatures. For comparative sketches, children seem to find it a help to have worksheets divided up into say four spaces with a title to each. This arrangement controls the size of the drawing and shows up what has (or has not) been filled in so far.

f. **Make notes** but *not* too much writing. The time at

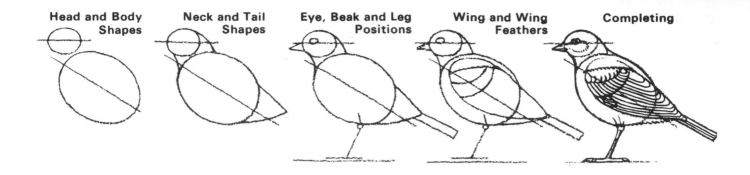

| Head and Body Shapes | Neck and Tail Shapes | Eye, Beak and Leg Positions | Wing and Wing Feathers | Completing |

the zoo is so limited, and the writing is so inconvenient; just quick notes to be used back in the classroom are all one should ask. If pupils have worksheets to fill in under the conditions around the sealion pool or in the aquarium, many of the girls at least will want a second copy when they get back, in order to make a neat one.

g. **Mark maps**   ready-printed maps of the world, to show where the zoo creatures live wild. On many cages there is a map with a coloured patch to show the homeland of the inmate. World maps can be rolled off in advance with a Mapograph roller (from Mapograph Co. Ltd. 440 High Road, London W.4) and dabs of felt-pen colour can be used to show habitats. Many children think of 'lions-and-tigers' as nextdoor neighbours, and of course in zoos they are just that. Pupils may also be surprised when they come to colour in the home areas of elephants. Some children have no idea that there can be two sorts. Others will sort out their ideas about crocodiles and alligators.

7 What can we do after we've been to the zoo?
Certainly there is, and should be, plenty of follow-up work. The occasion was too valuable to waste.

Questions and discussion first with reference books on the spot; nobody knows all the answers.

Then collecting observations with the teacher making the notes (as the one with the most practice in quick writing).

Perhaps now grouping the animals seen giving pupils the chance to suggest criteria for groups rather than sticking to the textbook 'bony fishes' or 'ruminants .

What about 'all the African animals', or 'all the creatures which can live in ice and snow all their lives' (North and South Poles), or 'all the creatures which go fishing'? So long as they work, in sorting creatures out into clear groups, the pupils' suggestions for criteria are helpful in getting them to understand the principles behind classification as a scientific process. This means something much more fundamental than just following the grouping in a zoology textbook, however valid.

Next, perhaps, come illustration and collage making   The postcards, and the illustrated books, prevent too much frustration among those for whom the drawing 'won't come right'. But *please* help these children to trace, if they must, in such a way that the book underneath is not ruined. A sharp pencil used lightly, and *not* a biro and carbon paper as seems to happen only too often with library books. Faber publish an attractive book by C. Cowell (1962) called *Your Book of Animal Drawing*, which, if it is available, should help them to draw British animals satisfactorily. The main problems are not in the kind of animal, but in factors such as that where we expect knees, horses already have ankles, and what in a horse looks like a knee, though in its front leg, is really its wrist. They all seem to a child to bend the wrong way. For those within reach of London, perhaps a visit to the Natural History Museum's skeletons of man and horse together would be right for the next excursion.

8 What science have we got from the zoo?
Observations and practice in observing. This is so important for science that it cannot be overemphasized as long as it remains enjoyable.

Knowledge gained from observing and from all the discussion and looking-up which result from the zoo and post zoo activities.

New ideas about classification, about ecology, about life under different conditions, about life cycles, about evolution, about adaptation and—important for some children—about the existence of other living creatures beyond themselves. There is little opportunity in a single visit for testing hypotheses, though if time allows there are many possibilities. As examples of starting points: heavy animals seem to have thick legs, or to live in water; or the animals which carry their babies in pouches all seem to come from Australia. Such ideas and hypotheses lead on to a general concept of pattern, and form the basis of much adult scientific work.

Using museums

Much of what applies to zoo visits applies here too. The preparations must be similar, with the exception that most museum work is indoors. It may be found more tiring, and is certainly better not taken in too large instalments. Seating and eating are both in the warm and dry, which is good.

Which museum is it to be? natural history or 'science' (better called history of technology)? Or perhaps a local exhibition of industrial archaeology? Man's inventions are often difficult to understand and less appealing than animals. The Children's Gallery has many 'fun things' in it, but again one may need to be literate and to have done some work on principles in order to make much use of what is presented.

The well informed and well prepared teacher is the key, and with such a person the class has a wonderful time, and comes back to make its own museum in the classroom: chicken and turkey skeletons, or working models of machines constructed from plastic Meccano, or collected paper aircraft (see *Aerial models*).

A collage of model aeroplanes against a clouded sky

7 What can we do about dinosaurs?

Children are fascinated by the name, the size (though they don't know how big they were) and the whole prehistoric picture. 'Mum, were you alive when dinosaurs were on the earth?' is not an invention. Children's sense of historical time develops so late that if they don't remember something themselves it simply happened before that.

What science can we look for in the dinosaur context? We think that as far as possible young pupils should have concrete experiences. Let us start by finding out the real sizes of a couple of favourites, say Brontosaurus, 20 metres long, and Tyrannosaurus, 15 metres long. Children may well know both of these by name. A good source of information is the Ladybird *Prehistoric Animals and Fossils*, chosen because children can have a copy themselves. With metre tapemeasure(s) and chalk, let's lay Brontosaurus and Tyrannosaurus on the line in the playground; they could be side by side (an unlikely situation, since the big one quietly ate plants, while the smaller one was more than likely to eat the bigger one). They could be arranged nose to nose if the playground space allows. Now for proportions. Pupils find the best side-view, and measure the lengths of head and neck, body, and tail separately. Another source of information is urgently needed, since Ladybird is no good here. Try *How and Why Wonder Book of Dinosaurs* by Transworld Publishing, 1976, the paper may be cheap, but the illustrations are a great help. Now all we have to do is to guess how fat these creatures were, using the pictures, and draw round our guess. Their weights are in the reference books too. If Bronto lived half in water perhaps this didn't worry him too much? Try modelling a large one in solid Plasticine, and feel how heavy it feels out of water, and then almost under water but not touching the bottom. Could the long neck have been a help too? (Why have it if it wasn't? might be a reasonable question.) There are many books on the subject for those who want to go further.

TYRANNOSAURUS REX

We should in any case have a look at these creatures' skeletons; after all, that's all we really have. An excursion to see them would be fine, but if not possible, then we should look at the best pictures we can find, remembering all the time those huge outlines in the playground.

Bones and skeletons

Colin, aged eleven, had to spend about six weeks in hospital. By the time he came out he had collected, with the friendly help of nurses and co-patients, an almost complete set of bones of one animal or another—lamb shoulder-blade, chicken everything but feet and skull, beef ribs etc, all shiny and (thanks to the nurses' anatomy classes) labelled. Birds' skulls are often found in the country or on the beach. If you know a butcher (or his child) you might get as a great favour the superb thigh-bone of a beef animal—to a child this is like a weight lifter's weight. The bones we find and collect are starting points for much measurement and comparison, especially with our own bones. 'Measuring me' is one of the most interesting things a younger child can do.

A skeleton of a horse

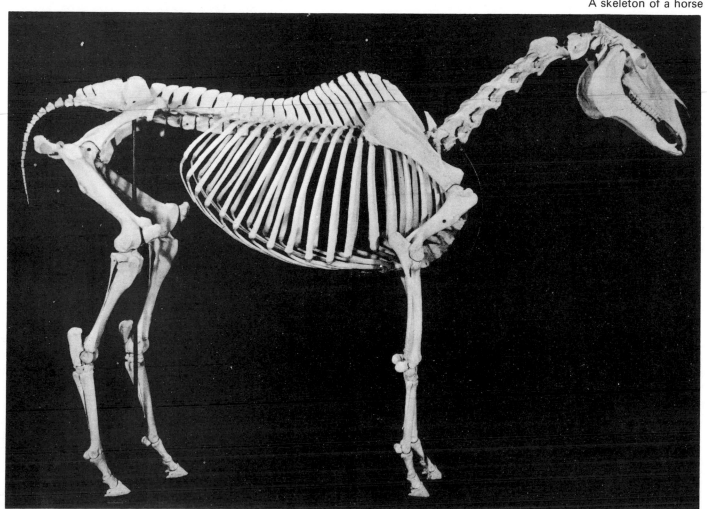

Miss, I can't find my wishbone. (Petra, aged eight). By good luck one of the boys had a little plastic skeleton in his case, and they could sort out the two collar bones which it (and therefore Petra) had instead. This then turned into a heated discussion about Rugby football, but more references to bones came into it, and these were also duly located. The quite amazing thing about comparing skeletons is that there are so many similarities: bats with their long fingers, frogs short only of thumbs, horses walking on their middle 'finger-nails' and 'toe-nails', and so on.

Have your pupils drawn round their other hand? And counted the bones? And found out by experiment why there are creases at the knuckles? And measured each finger? And measured the furthest they can stretch along a ruler from fingertip to thumbtip? And found out the figures for the rest of the class? And thought why this might be important, and to whom? And measured to see why handcuffs won't come off? This will go on for a long time if you want it to, and any friendly or well known animal pets can join in, with feet as well as hands. Perhaps some of the class can add their feet outlines for homework? A collage is easy, fun and important in focussing information; the prehistoric creatures deserve one too. A book called *How to Draw Prehistoric and Mythical Animals* by A. Zaidenberg (Abelard-Schuman, 1968) will be a great help. For a superb collection of first class drawings of skeletons of today's common animals, cow, cat, squirrel, tortoise, frog, fish and many others, use *Clue Book Bones*, by G. Allen & J. Denslow (Oxford University Press, 1968/70).

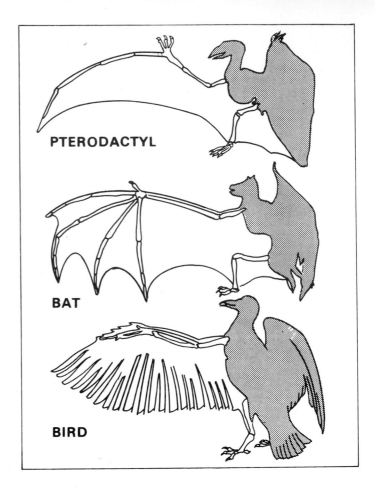

PTERODACTYL

BAT

BIRD

8 Collectors and collections

Professor Peter Medawar says that 'Scientists include collectors, detectives, explorers, artists, and artisans.' What is scientific about collecting? The subtitle of Piaget and Inhelder's book *The early growth of logic in the child* is *Classification and Seriation*. Mary Sime, in her delightful book *Child's Eye View*, paraphrases Piaget: 'The skill to classify (and the skill to seriate) are the two roots of logical thinking that are the first to develop in the human being.' And before anyone can practise the skill of classification there has to be material to look at, to compare, to think about—someone has had to collect it.

Gerry brought back from his summer holiday at the seaside a large plastic bag of shells he personally had collected for pleasure. Gerry was only six at the time and therefore at either the stage Piaget calls pre-classification or at the next stage, quasi-classification. But even at the first of these, though the objects are only seen as a visual pattern, with adult help he can do some useful sorting. At the next stage (usually from about five to seven years old) children can be very good at sorting so long as only one criterion at a time is used. Gerry himself had had conversation with adults on the beach, though they had not given him any 'training' in sorting. He divided his shells into the 'sea snails', eg winkles, whelks etc. and the 'scoop shells', eg cockles, limpets, mussels and razorshells, because this is what he had used them for on the sand. His classification groups are interesting, because the first depends on a property of the shell, which is a more advanced criterion, while the second depends primarily on a use, though this in turn is a property of the shape of the shell, since snail-type shells are not very good scoops.

Mary Sime, working on the Piaget basis, says that 'true classification is a potent intellectual tool once it is firmly developed', but that a teacher can only ensure that a child will have a firm foundation for this development by giving him plentiful practice through which he can exercise these developing skills. But plenty of adults still make collections, and of all sorts of the oddest (and maybe unscientific) objects. Why? A main reason among the very young, and the very young at heart, is simple acquisition—perhaps just to have large numbers. This is followed by very personal reactions: the biggest, the prettiest, the smallest or (slightly more mature) the rarest. Children show all of these to varying degrees with teddies, marbles, stamps, Matchbox or Dinky cars, and the advance in their development shows, whatever the material.

Adults as well as children may collect 'something other people haven't got', for example, the adult collectors of snuffboxes, glass paperweights or old bottles. Some adults, and occasionally children too, look for a cash value, either from a large number of one kind of object (see auctioneers' catalogues) or from rarities. They may not intend to sell them, but simply to treasure something which has a high cash or antique value for the primitive satisfaction of possession, or perhaps a social status.

The real scientist sorts objects and material into sets, collecting only one or a few of each, but of as many variations on the chosen theme as possible. 'Spotters' may be considered to have developed the 'purest' form of collection, since no spotting takes the object away from others, nor can there be any cash value on a sighting, whether of rare bird or of rare locomotive.

What science can we help junior pupils to derive from this common and obviously pleasurable activity of collecting? Teaching Primary Science *Seeds and seedlings* makes several suggestions: collected seeds can be classified into important sets—by uses, by type of distribution, and by internal structure; a collection is also valuable for reference when other collectors have seeds which they wish to identify. Different criteria chosen for the groups in this sorting process provide the children working on the material with a great opportunity for producing their own ideas, and this leads them towards flexible thinking, and the fact that maybe there is more than 'one right answer'. So long as the criterion does its job of helping to sort accurately, then it's a 'right' answer. In *Seeds and seedlings* collections are also suggested as ways of extending factual knowledge, eg the pictures on seed packets, food packs and food cans show children what wheat-ears, peapods and mangoes look like. There are many small children who think that peas are little round green things which come out of a deep-freeze in plastic bags.

Other books in the Teaching Primary Science series give more example of the uses of collections. *Paints and materials* for example, shows how leaves can be collected for shape, colour, size etc. Furthermore, pupils may find out ways of recording them, by outline, making

Taking a rubbing of a manhole cover with a wax crayon (Permission should be obtained before taking rubbings in churches.)

leaf-prints, silhouettes, and rubbings. These methods can then be extended to the recording of other surfaces in a more complex way, such as rubbing with added colour-wash. This technique leads on to a study of the waterproofing quality of wax, and so on. In *Aerial models* a collection of folded paper planes is suggested to illustrate the comparison of effects of a single variable, a concept for older juniors which is made comprehensible by personal experiment with the paper.

Organization of collections for use

Short term storage space is probably the first essential, and needs to be found in advance. Plastic bags with the usual closures can be hung from small hooks on pegboard against the wall. This keeps the material from being lost or ignored, and is more convenient than boxes, as the contents can be seen without taking off any lids. Sorting for example, a collection of autumn seeds, acorns, conkers, sycamore 'spinners' etc, is best done into a set of identical containers such as margarine tubs. In this way younger children, who are likely to be doing

Fold 3 paper gliders all alike and try the effect of adding paperclips

1 paperclip on the front end

2 paper clips underneath

2 paperclips on the back

DO THEY FLY BETTER OR WORSE?

this simple classification, only have one criterion—the kind of seed—in front of them. It's 'conker' or 'acorn', not 'does this one go into the yoghurt pot or the little bucket?'

We can display the material immediately the sorting is finished but then only for a short time, because as we all

43

know, the material gets dusty and nobody 'sees' it anyway. Closed transparent containers are greatly preferable to any other sort. Jars are good if kept safely on a shelf; clear plastic lunch boxes (as supplied by Stewart Plastics of Purley Way, Croydon, for example) are excellent. They have many other uses as well, such as making child-sized aquaria for close observation of water snails, tadpoles etc. The lids are important for collection display, as without them, conkers etc, tend to disappear.

Stamp zoo

This is a collecting activity with many advantages. Many countries, including Great Britain, produce first class pictures of animals on their stamps. These can be made into most attractive display collections, with extension possibilities into ecology, geography and mathematics. A large plan of the local or London zoo can be used as a background for a collage. Classify the animals on the stamps according to classes, reptiles, fishes, mammals etc. A large map of the world can be used as a basis for the grouping of creatures into geographical areas. Some of the more sensitive children prefer this to a zoo, and like to place the animals where they live in the wild. However, a Pets' Corner is then needed for poodles and pekinese!

Methuen's Children's Books Series (1973) includes a very attractive World of Stamps volume called *Domestic Animals*, which gives children ideas about both collecting and classifying, using minimal text and good illustrations. Security is a problem with stamps. Young children glue their stamps in ways which fanatic philatelists can't bear to watch, but these stamps are fairly safe from inquisitive or acquisitive fingers. However, the older enthusiast needs more professional standards. Probably the best way to make everybody happy is to use stamp hinges as in albums. For a good display, hinge the stamps on good paper, and mount behind glass in a large picture frame. Such frames may be found in many lofts, or cheaply in secondhand shops. The right ones for the purpose have wooden or hardboard backs, and usually have some means of fixing the backing into the frame, so that nothing can go wrong.

Children, and their parents, are good at suggesting ways to overcome practical problems, and very often they will supply the means to the end, especially if it stemmed originally from their own suggestion.

9 Exhibitions and displays

What are the special reasons for making displays and exhibitions in science work?

1 Because science deals with real things. Children in junior and middle school age-ranges are very largely still in the concrete stages of development, and need things in order to understand about them. Even adults learning about new materials do it much more successfully if they are given the concrete objects to begin with.

Each child's own limited supply of particular items— sea shells, seeds or springs—can be extended by adding to it those of others in the class. Occasional extras from the teacher may have been chosen to add breadth and excitement, but the main show must be the children's own, or they will have far less personal interest in the whole affair.

2 An exhibition or display gives as many children as possible a chance to 'matter', to have a little limelight. In collecting 'scientific' objects, say cockle shells, or different kinds of metal, the pupil who is not academically able may prove to be a wizard on the beach or in the workshop. A display organized with enthusiasm can provide motivation for both the over-quiet reader and the over-active non reader to practise scientific skills, perhaps both together. Many children learn a lot from visual stimuli, and can get help from others in doing so, though they may take in almost nothing from looking at text.

3 The exhibition is a source of real material for class exercises in science and mathematics: for observation, identification and recognition; for comparison, grouping and classification; for the discovery of patterns. Measuring and arrangement in series may be relevant, while extensions into craftwork, art and writing are sure to be available and to some extent necessary.

4 Setting up a class or group display involves communication—a stimulus to the class members and to outsiders. Other classes or groups may wish to visit and/or emulate, and parents will be pleased and perhaps encouraged to add further material and expertise. The teacher, however keen and able, should not do it all; lending a hand here and there is different.

Lifespan of an exhibition

The one thing to avoid is staleness: 'We've finished this. What do we do next?' is an only too well known child comment. Maybe we can take a few good photographs as a permanent reminder of a happy event; one or two black-and-white exposures for enlargement, and a few colour slides taken with flash for slide projection. After that we rapidly return borrowed items to owners, and put anything we can genuinely use for reference into storage boxes with labels. Children's own work needs to be considerately treated, but much of the collection material can disappear, with permission of the one-time owner who has got the satisfaction out of seeing it on show. End of week or end of term clearing-up means more space for new science next week or next term.

Setting up a science display

Essentials
1 A clear theme such as paper gliders, or seeds. A clear message is the most important idea, since any display can easily be cluttered up with irrelevant items contributed by the more 'grasshopper-minded'. Scientific patterns at different levels could be selected for a display of seeds, for example: (a) seeds found in the

playground *(b)* some seeds which grow in pods *(c)* some seeds which grow inside juicy fruits *(d)* seeds which are the main food grains of the world.

2 Clear display methods

These might include *(a)* ways of raising some objects for good viewing, since table tops and shelves are very flat; *(b)* ways of fixing objects in position with, for example, small spots of rub-off glue (Copydex or Cowgum) or Blutak; *(c)* ways of labelling, such as coloured yarn from object to well-lettered card; the card can be lettered with a plastic letter-stencil ruler; *(d)* using trays, eg the plastic type which previously contained rows of yoghurt pots or peaches. These are excellent for small items such as sea shells which can otherwise become completely jumbled on a table top or large tray.

3 Clear space

for such display depends on the classroom furniture: a good shelf, or tables against the wall, or a glass-fronted cupboard.

Using wall space

Clear space on walls is often as hard to find as space on the flat. However, objects can be very effectively displayed by mounting them on vertical pegboard with wire hooks or rubber bands, or on expanded polystyrene ceiling tiles with pins. The backing sheet can also be hung up if fixing is undesirable.

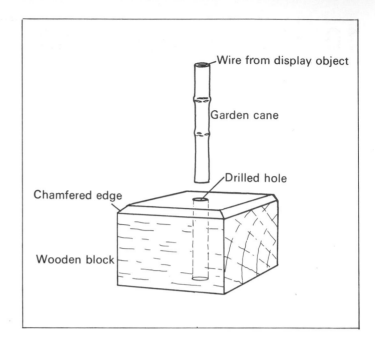

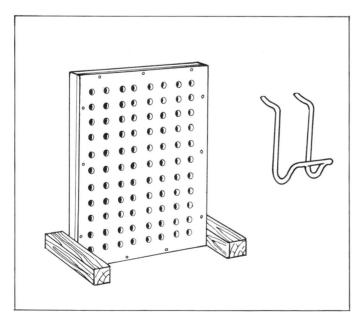

Netlon-type netting holds larger objects so that they can be seen in three dimensions, or single items can be fixed on top of either stiff wire or thin dowel rod, the bottom end being held by a wood or metal base, or by a jar of sand or pebbles. Collages form an additional opportunity to extend a display of solid objects, eg a seaside view with fish and crabs etc in the water to add a new dimension to shells and pebbles collected by the pupils. Small collages show up well on a folding pegboard screen, either the zigzag type or the triptych (sides into the middle) version. Both kinds have the advantage that they can be folded up, with or without the collages, for immediate space-clearing or storage. Children usually enjoy collages because they can all share in the making; they can take you, or a parent, up to the display and point out their fish in the sea, their musical instrument among the guitars, their bronto among the prehistoric animals.

Suggestions for displays and collages can be found in Teaching Primary Science *Musical instruments, Fibres and fabrics, Aerial models* and *Seeds and seedlings.* Many suggestions for material to be collected and exhibited are to be found in Science 5/13 *Using the environment 1 Early Explorations* (pp. 28-46).

10 Mathematics and 'right answers'

It is impossible to say where science ends and mathematics begins; science always needs mathematics In the books of this series *Teaching Primary Science* we use numbers and we group into sets, drawing Venn diagrams. We measure length, area (by counting squares), volume, mass, time and angles. We deal a number of times with reflection and symmetry, we use simple mathematical methods of recording in graphical form, and we arrange, for example, musical instruments in order of size—from shortest or smallest to longest or largest, correlating their dimensions with the pitch of the notes they produce (even in hertz, or vibrations per second).

How can we best help children to use and to enjoy using these mathematical skills and processes in science work?

a. Perhaps by making sure ourselves that the mathematics will be relevant rather than routine. Barry (aged eight), asked by his mother why he didn't want to take his precious new hamster to school: 'Well, we'd only have to weigh it, measure it, draw it and write about it.' On the other hand, John (aged ten) on the beach: 'Our class teacher brought us down here last year to find shells, and when we took them back and measured them, mine was the biggest cockle, and it measured seven centimetres across.

b. We can make each bit of mathematical process as concrete, visual and direct as possible. For example, sort real seeds into sets and a Venn diagram made of loops of coloured string; measure the rolling distance of a marble on the floor with a tape measure rather than

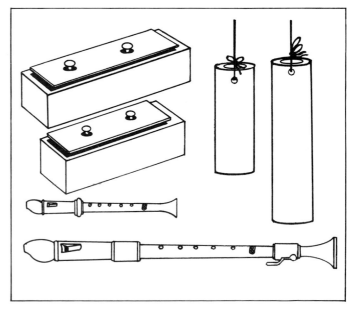

with string which itself then has to be measured; find the wing area of a paper plane by using a transparent plastic centimetre squared grid and counting the squares.

c. We can try to avoid arithmetical calculations until we know for certain that the pupils have learnt how to do them and understand what they mean. It is so easy to think that a proportion sum is just obvious, but to many children it is nothing of the sort, and a quick 'explanation in order to get the answer we need, gives the child the rather common feeling that arithmetic is a secret which grown-ups keep to themselves.

d. For just this reason we can make an extra effort to co-ordinate work with other teachers taking mathematics, so that everyone helps everyone else, and maths in science lessons is not so different from maths in maths lessons as sometimes happens.

Right answers

It may be the case that in arithmetic there *is* only one right answer, but this is certainly not true in the sciences. However, the feeling that the one and only right answer is expected is, as Edward de Bono points out, a potent reason for pupils' later insecurity and unhappiness in mathematics and physics. Many teachers recognize the symptoms, even in themselves, perhaps when dealing with 'new mathematics' for the first time. So when children ask 'What ought it to do?' in a science experiment, perhaps the best answer is simply 'Don't ask me, let's ask the experiment.' And this is in any case one of the most suitably scientific ways to deal with any problem.

Then we can find ways of demonstrating that it works. Have a number of pupils make a measurement— especially a biological one—and let every child notice the values carefully. They will not all be the same, whether it is heartbeats per half minute, one week's growth of a maize seedling, the volume of 100 soaked peas, or the weights of siblings in a litter of gerbils all born in the same half hour. In these cases this difference is not revealing the apparent inefficiency of any child, but the fact that the material does not always give you the same answer to the same question. This is fine for

the morale of the experimenter, but warns him or her to keep a very close watch on nature. This is the essence of being a good scientist.

Looking for explanations

In several books in the Teaching Primary Science series, examples are given of children's attempts to find reasons for unexpected or new results. It is very important to give them the chance and the motivation to look for such explanations, though our own may be quite different. Children have to learn to think, and to practise thinking, which they can't do if we always rush at them with our adult 'right answer'. A very good example is given in *Candles* where Elizabeth (aged five) sees melted candle wax dripping from the top of a lighted candle held slanting downwards, and suggests that the liquid comes out of a very small hole by the wick. She is almost certainly comparing the candle with a washing-up liquid bottle. Some experiments later, she realized that the candle actually got shorter, not emptier . . . but she had to do the thinking, observing, experimenting and measuring, for the experience to have any real value.

Thinks . . .

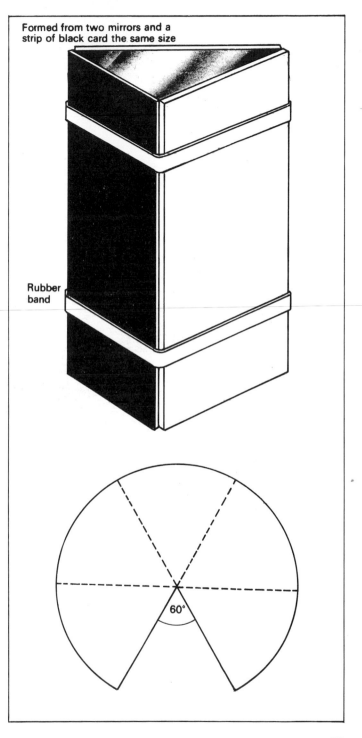

Formed from two mirrors and a strip of black card the same size

Rubber band

Two simple mathematical examples mentioned but not worked out, in other books in the series are: in *Science from wood* a pupil is numbering the rings on a nice clear log of Wiltshire treetrunk (page 24). 'We think the tree was 10 years old' was the decision; but do we know for certain that this log came from the very bottom of the tree? It could have been a piece out of a big branch from a hundred-year old tree. And for a second, different example, in *Mirrors and magnifiers* we all observe that if two flat mirrors face inwards at an angle of 60° with a small 'pattern' between them, we see the same pattern six times round a circle, counting the real object. Now wait a minute, there is one real object, so we must be seeing five images. But both of the mirrors do the same thing—each gives us an image of the real thing seen in the mirror (that makes a total of three). Then each mirror gives us an image of what it catches from the other mirror; that makes two more, total five. But there's no space in the middle at the back of the kaleidoscope pattern. Each mirror goes one step further, and gives us an image of what we saw the first time—each mirror giving us back its own first-time image as it caught it from its partner (a second-time reflection). Both mirrors are exactly alike, and do exactly the same thing. This seems to mean that we should have one real object and *six* (2+2+2) images.

It is comforting to know (and to be able to check this by drawing it) that the two second-time images, one from each mirror, are exactly alike, and come neatly on top of one another round there at the back of the pattern. So they look like one image. This should perhaps look brighter than the others, but glass absorbs some light, and by the second time of reflection both images have got fainter, so we don't see that there are two on top of one another.

Of course this is not necessary knowledge for children. We would not think of 'teaching it to them', but it is just possible that some serious pupil might ask about it. (See *Mirrors and magnifiers*, pp. 14-15).

A mathematician's problem

It is often very difficult for a top-level mathematician to see what it is that a child does not understand. Piaget's work shows up this kind of problem in quite small everyday things. We would all take it for granted that a mugful of water doesn't actually swell when we tip it into a tall narrow jar, and get smaller again as we tip it back into the mug. But to the young child—even a child of school age—this is by no means so obvious. The water comes up higher in the narrow jar, so there must be more of it. And the designers of shampoo and salad dressing bottles work on the assumption that some of us, the purchasing public, are still influenced by the same idea.

In the book *Science from water play* many experiences are suggested to try to help children past this stage. Pouring water to and fro, marking levels, using jars of different shapes but the same capacity. As with so much of our work in science, the mathematical comprehension children need really only comes from a large number of slightly different experiences, with the same basic idea behind them (ie in the teacher's mind). We are not 'telling them'—that does not work; we are providing

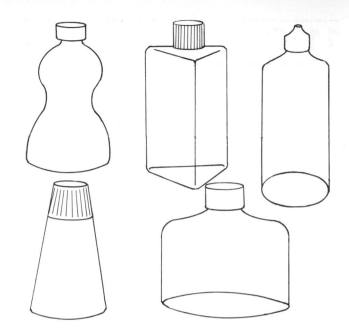

as much guided discovery as we can possibly put into their activities without the pressure which raises emotional barriers. For young children the 'right answer' from us has no real meaning, but it may well stop them from trying, and therefore prevent them from finding out for themselves.

Sometimes we have to offer a suggestion with a straight face. A group of children were measuring the length of the corridor outside their classroom, but seemed to be having difficulties. After some conversation they came back to report that they couldn't do it; the teacher asked why not (they had taken rulers with them). They said: 'We took our own rulers, and we borrowed as many as we could from the next class but we still haven't got enough to reach from one end to the other.' This is a case for the 'Could you . . .' or 'Would it be an idea to . . .' kind of hint. Then the children see it for themselves and laugh at themselves. They have really learnt something and will never make this mistake again.

11 Cooking: an interest of children and adults

Cooking makes a superb introduction to a wide range of scientific activities. Current trends are for younger as well as older pupils to do some cookery in school, and for men to teach it as well as women, so the opportunities increase.

What, apart from a gratifying if short-lived end product, can we derive from cookery in the way of science? Here are some suggestions; there are many more which turn up all the time, though not all of them are as suitable for younger pupils—often because of the need for high temperatures and therefore the danger that goes with them.

1 Observations, using several senses

A wide selection of observations about properties of materials can be made by the youngest pupils. These involve several senses which is particularly valuable, since elsewhere observations tend to be purely visual.

Try the *smells* of grated lemon peel or peppermint flavouring; the *feel* of coarse sugar crystals or fine flour, the stinging sensation of chopped onion to the eyes (while the chopping is going on—don't rub it in); the *taste* of salt or the tastelessness of plain flour; the *sound* of tapping on over-toasted toast.

None of these observations needs to be made into a formal test. Making such things formal detaches them from real life. They are best as part of an apparently spontaneous but guided discovery, as suggested by the teacher who has objectives in mind during the cooking processes.

2 Experience of materials

Cooking uses a fine range of substances to be studied and enjoyed; some children will have the background of 'helping Mum', but for others school is able to give more freedom as well as help.
Obvious substances to be investigated include:
Powders eg flour, custard powder, cocoa, icing sugar.
Crystals eg salt, and various kinds of sugar.
> Preserving sugar is particularly good, as the well-shaped crystals are large enough to be seen separately. (Children may think of loaf sugar, but of course the 'cubes' are cut out of masses of small crystals stuck together—this is something the pupils can study too.)

Liquids eg 'runny' eg water, milk, colourings, essences.
> 'thick' eg syrup, honey. (The effect of warming these in a bowl standing in hot water is of interest too, both in cooking and in science.)

Halfway substances between liquid and solid eg jelly. (Again, there are several important phenomena to be seen, both when jellies are warmed—say jelly marmalade—and when they are diluted, from blocks or dried 'crystals', say—when making table jellies.)

Fats eg butter, margarine. The effects of heat are once more of importance from both angles. Also the fact that fat or oil does not mix with water makes a striking contrast with most of the other substances involved in cooking.

And then there are all the materials which come in small solid 'pieces' such as coconut and cake fruit.

The list above supposes a simple form of sorting or

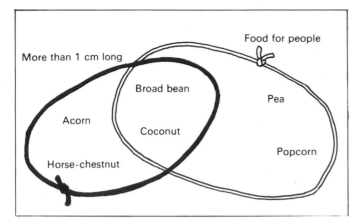

classification. You may like to suggest to pupils that they think out ways of classifying what they use in their activities—sweet, salt, sour, what needs cooking, what doesn't need cooking etc. The more valid criteria they think of for classification the better.

3 Weighing and measuring

Many mothers do their cooking by what looks to the child like guesswork, they do not realize how much experience lies behind it. However, they may well protest that they do not need to weigh materials if Mum doesn't. Would you think it worth trying a little experiment in which one group follows the recipe and a parallel group just guesses? It will not automatically show that weighing is best—one class which did this experiment found that they liked the guesswork cake better than the book version, because the boy doing the sugar-guessing just tipped up the packet to his own satisfaction.

At the moment in Britain there is a different problem over cookery quantities which must be taken quite seriously, especially by teachers thinking about the science involved. This is the question of metric and old standard units. We have many packets which now give metric quantity first and the 'old' quantity second, but recipe books are not as frequently reprinted as sugar packets. The whole approach needs careful thought and discussion with other colleagues, especially in mathematics, so that the pupils get the help they need in this rather difficult transition. Perhaps the table-spoonful still has something to be said for it?

4 Processes to study

These are interesting to study because things happen. You only have to make a list to see this: mix, dissolve, melt, stir, beat, whisk, roll out, grease, spread, heat, bake, cool, ice; boil, toast, scramble, dust with icing sugar, and so on. Enough to make one's mouth water. And children need as well as enjoy these words; they are not just 'something teacher says we have to learn'. They are real, and good preparation for vocabulary pages in the cooking files. The processes they name are all going to be used again and again, the skills will be learnt and practised. Some occur in science lessons later on, but even more will come in handy in the home, flat or bed-sitter.

Now for the effects resulting from some of these processes. This is where the older juniors begin to understand fully that results have causes, and that neither wishing nor magic saves your cakes if you forget about them in the oven.

There are so many valid tests to try as well as things to make that one has to choose a few which are of general importance.

Many other examples are worth trying, eg brown sugar, which gives two proofs that it has spread right through

250 grams
icing sugar

1 egg

peppermint essence

a little water

Peppermint Creams
Collect all these things
to make your peppermint creams.
Put the sugar in a bowl.

the water. Cake-icing colourings are good as soluble examples, because one can see the coloured liquid actually mixing with the colourless water in beautiful trails. Luckily the bottles in which these colourings are sold usually have one-drop-at-a-time stoppers. Salt should be good for dissolving, as well as being cheap, but the results will in fact be muddling, because of the (harmless) powder added to make it run smoothly out of the salt-pourer. This makes it look cloudy and white, spoiling the 'soluble' picture.

2 Toasting

What about toasting, for everyday effects of both sight and smell? Drying, browning, singeing, burning, blackening are all possible results. These can't all be seen in the oven, where the safety risk is too great, but with a sensible child-height grill so that children need not climb, small squares of bread can be given the full treatment. Mum will probably hear about it that evening, too. And a whole set of facts will drop into place with the 'ah-ha' phenomenon.

3 Thickening

The fascinating process resulting in the 'thickening' of flour paste, porridge, custard or even instant mashed potato, is another of these common events which repay closer study. It does involve boiling water (milk is more risky with its tendency to boil over suddenly), but the teacher's demonstration in a large Pyrex bowl seen from the sides is convincing. Spoonfuls of the result cool quickly, and the flour paste can be compared for effective stickiness with the cold mixture (and with Polycell, which is similar to but works better than the edible flour paste).

4 Change in taste

is naturally one of the most important general effects of cooking. Try this by comparing the taste of raw potato with that of well boiled potato or instant mash. Children will suggest other examples which they have themselves tried— some of which we would hardly propose to the class.

5 The setting of egg-white

(and yolk) is a result of a cooking process which is taken for granted. Cracking the egg on the edge of a glass bowl and sliding it into a poacher, or omelette pan of boiling water (better because it is more spreadout), lets the pupils really observe that the uncooked white is not yet white, but is clear, colourless and transparent. Another egg cracked on to a patterned plate shows the pattern

through the white—and this egg can be the next to cook. The changes as it becomes hot are visible, definite, and happen slowly enough for them to be recorded. It is clear that it is the boiling water which turns the transparent 'white' into an opaque truly white solid. Slide a poached egg (even better, the same one) on to the patterned plate, and try to see the pattern through it now. (See section 1 above, too.)

Don't worry about the biochemistry of the egg proteins which goes on, just keep an eye on the egg.

Precautions

Naturally cooking has its dangers, but children can learn with and from you how to avoid them. Overheated chip pans of oil form the greatest fire hazard in home kitchens, so they should be kept out of cookery areas for juniors, as should any kind of cooking which can 'spit'. It is not worth taking this kind of risk.

Some of the children's books about cooking try to work mainly with cold foods, and several find peppermint creams, coconut ice or various salads to be safe suggestions. There isn't much science here, though, nor in fact much cookery.

Sweets and snacks (a Macdonald Starter) gives simple recipes for children, but the so-called 'reminder' to wear oven gloves before touching hot trays and dishes comes right at the end . . .

We should take this idea seriously. Some of the bought oven gloves are far from heat-proof, and perhaps it would be wise to help children to make effective gloves in child sizes, with long cuffs to protect small wrists. *NB* A plastic sponge is not very safe—some kinds just melt.

The science from oven glove protection is of course all about heat insulation, though we are usually more anxious to keep heat in than to keep it away from ourselves (eg eiderdowns or fibreglass in lofts). However, this shows again that the topic of cooking leads to many different aspects of science. You, or you and your pupils, may like to make a flowchart of some of the possibilities: the metals for pans, the methods of heating, the kinds of food material, and so on. It may take a large sheet of paper.

12 Colours and science

Colour is one of the most enjoyable topics for any age group. There are so many ways in which it is involved in things which look interesting. Since there are books full of ideas eg Science 5/13 *Coloured things* and Teaching Primary Science *Paints and materials* let us consider mainly practical points.

1 The overhead projector again. Writing and drawing can be brilliantly coloured if the correct felt tipped pens are used. Coloured film can be bought to stick on the acetate sheets, but since quite small areas are big enough, cellophane sweet wrappings are quite practical, stuck down with rubber-type gum eg

putting a colour wash over a white candle resist

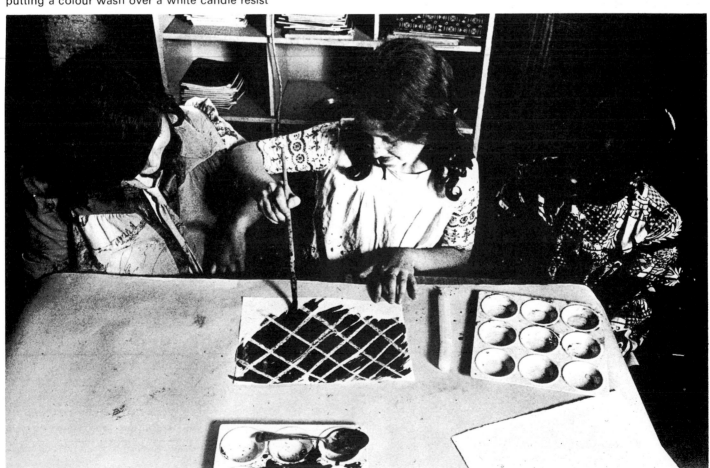

Copydex for easy removal. Whole collages can be built up from almost nothing, at no cost. Each wrapping must be tested first on the projector, as some which look bright by reflected light (the usual way) come out black on the projector screen (ie they do not let any light through). This is also a piece of science.

2 Beams of coloured light
For many important experiments with mirrors and the way light is reflected, one or two electric torches with coloured glass, cellophane or acetate over the front are very useful. In passing, children could well start by taking the battery out of a torch, checking where the two contacts are made, how the switch makes and breaks the circuit, and how to put it all together again. This is good practice. The simple coloured beam tests can go like this: look at the light from the torch; then look at it with a piece of coloured film (eg E. J. Arnold acetate sheet for cutting up comes in six colours) or the right sweet wrapping in front of the glass. The colour that you see is the one which has come through, obviously. So the coloured film is a colour(ed) filter. Next shine the beam from the torch on to a matt white wall or piece of paper without filter. Guess what will happen when you put the filter in front, then try it. This technique of going a little way with instructions, and then beginning to *make guesses* (hypotheses) and *check* them is fine for building up children's skill and confidence in scientific method; so often they only need a start from us.

3 Reflection
Now shine the coloured beam of light (from torch through acetate) at a mirror, at an angle of roughly 45° to the glass. Ask someone else to look in the mirror from the other side of the middle, and to move until they can see the coloured beam coming from the mirror as if the torch were shining straight at their eyes (see diagram 1). Trying this with different angles, different colours and even different torches— perhaps two pairs of children working on the same mirror at the same time (see diagram 2)—provides experiences for the 'ah-ha!' phenomenon, in which one or more pupils may suddenly 'see' the main law of reflection, about which nobody has said a word. Don't tell them, let them find out. And don't let anybody make them do 'mirrors and pins' experiments instead. (See *Mirrors and magnifiers*, p. 25).

4 Rainbow colours—the spectrum
There are few experiences in science more impressive than a brilliant display of the colours of the rainbow. Sir Isaac Newton and Noah shared this feeling with us. Children standing in the sunshine at a classroom window with triangular glass or plastic prisms can make a wonderful display on the ceiling. But prisms are expensive; so keep handy, ready for the moments of instant sunshine, a few flat (plane) mirrors (E. J. Arnold or Osmiroid plastic ones are unbreakable) to stand slanting in shallow water in the sun. See Ladybird: *Light, Mirrors and Lenses* for the method, although their results are rather optimistic. Somebody always recites the 'seven colours of the rainbow/spectrum'. Are there really seven? Isn't indigo just dark blue? Maybe there are six, and one was put in to make up the 'special' number? Rainbow colours round the classroom are easy to organize. Using tiny pots of touch-up enamel,

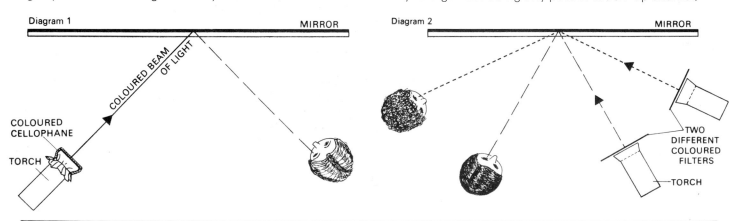

Diagram 1

MIRROR

COLOURED BEAM OF LIGHT

COLOURED CELLOPHANE

TORCH

Diagram 2

MIRROR

TWO DIFFERENT COLOURED FILTERS

TORCH

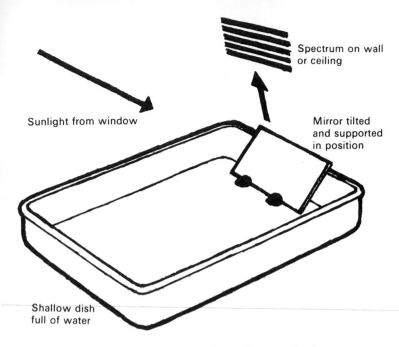

Spectrum on wall or ceiling

Sunlight from window

Mirror tilted and supported in position

Shallow dish full of water

paint them on to say tray-ends or drawers, in the correct order, and the order sticks without meaningless mnemonics.

5 Coloured filters

cut out other colours. Take some coloured acetate—red, blue, green—and cut 5-cm squares. Look at the window through one blue square, then two, then three, all on top of one another—it gets darker, doesn't it? So a filter cuts out some light. Now try looking at a bright picture—red, blue, green, yellow etc—through a red square. What has happened to the green bits? They have gone black? Try the green square on the same picture; what's happened to the red bits? Have they gone black now? Make a guess about what the red bits will look like through a blue filter—and test your guess. *NB* The picture colours need to be 'crude'—the same sort of colours as those of the acetate. It is worth looking at Christmas packing papers etc to find the 'right' thing. Pastel shades don't help at all.

6 'Look out!' and 'Danger!' colours

Why do the men on the railway line wear orange waistcoats? What colour are the stripes on the back of a 'long load' truck? Some colours show up better in poor light. This topic provides many chances for children to experiment and learn—for life.

13 Magnets

There are four ways of looking at science work with children:
1 Picking up practical skills and practising them, for examples see chapters 4 and 11, and also Teaching Primary Science *Science from wood, Paints and materials, Aerial models.*

Using a bench-hook

2 Sorting out and arranging material in organized ways
See chapters 6 and 8, and also Teaching Primary Science *Seeds and seedlings* or *Fibres and fabrics.*

3 Testing materials and ideas, and making the tests 'fair'. See Teaching Primary Science *Candles, Aerial models* and *Science from wood.*

4 Carrying out activities which lead to knowledge of scientific facts. See Teaching Primary Science *Musical Instruments, Science from waterplay, Mirrors and magnifiers,* and *Seeds and seedlings.*

Work with magnets

This chapter specially stresses activities in the last group, and here there is a great deal which even young children can find out and learn. Primary science is not, and should not be, concerned with learning 'Laws'. It provides experiences to give children a stock of discovered facts; on these they can build later.

Discovery experiences

'Miss, tell us what we're supposed to do.'
A situation in which children are as free to try tests and experiments as the building materials and peer-group allow is an interesting one-off event for the thoughtful teacher. However, most young children are unable to use such an opportunity fully, if at all. This may be due to lack of previous 'free' experience, to lack of knowledge of the possibilities, or simply to lack of confidence. Moreover, the discoveries the more capable children do make, though exciting, are usually unorganized, isolated, and often too difficult to explain. Hence these children become confused and lose impetus, while their classmates have nothing to show for the time spent.

Guided discovery

This chapter on work with magnets follows much modern educational thought by suggesting many small experiments grouped into a definite progression—a kind of extended check list for the teacher. It makes it possible for the pupils to discover step by step, with the teacher never telling them what the answer should be before they have had a chance to find out. Of course it does not prevent them from discovering ahead of time. But every child, even the slowest, is able to take part.

Three hints:
a. Tapping, hitting or dropping magnets weakens magnets.
b. Iron filings make a very unpleasant mess. If you feel you must use them, then keep them in sealed plastic boxes.
c. Leave 'fields of force' till the CSE and O-level years, when children are old enough to deal with abstractions.

Magnetic attraction

The main kind of magnets that pupils will bring into the classroom, from the age of five onwards, will be horseshoe magnets. Attraction is the thing horseshoe magnets do best; in fact, it is the only thing they do well. However, it is and should be 'number one' experience. A class will need as many magnets as possible, since everybody wants to try everything. The small 'chunky' horseshoe type (Eclipse, Alnico etc) are better than the longer flat ones. Some apparently horseshoe type magnets can be bought cheaply for cupboard-door catches.

Attraction experiments
1 Test the magnet against large objects around the classroom, eg waterpipes, window catches etc, for the 'feel' of attraction, or lack of it.

2 Try picking up small specially chosen objects such as nails, panel pins, hairgrips, and particularly the common wire paperclips. These are excellent material for other tests and experiments, and may with luck be obtained from the school office. *NB* collect them up at the end. Little boys' pockets often contain 'prestige-length' chains of them when the raw material is available, and for small girls shorter chains serve as jewellery.

Pulling these objects off the magnet is also a good experience.

3 Test the picking-up action when the magnet is held just above, but not touching, the same objects. At this stage this is a kind of magic—action at a distance can't really be explained yet.

4 Experiment with the pulling-along effect, using the magnet horizontally.

5 Try also drawing a magnet across a table, pulling a nose-to-tail touching, but not linked, train of paperclips.

6 Compare strengths of different magnets, either in pairs or as a series, by feel as in **2**, and by rough measurements using **3** and **5**; ie how high, and how many?

7 Test attraction through materials: paper, card, plastic, fabric, thin wood (say matchbox or ply), kitchen aluminium foil (pie cases etc). Firstly with the magnet above (picking up), and then with it below, eg making paperclips move around in a foil flan case, or making them move up the inside of a plastic coffee beaker with the magnet outside.

Magnet games

The activities described, especially 5 and 7, are already 'natural' games, in spite of also being basic physics demonstrations. Here are some other examples but of a more 'invented' nature.

Treasure hunt On a fairly large plastic tray, put one (or more) steel washers of the kind used in mathematics, and cover the whole bottom of the tray with a generous layer of clean dry sawdust. The 'detector' is of course a small strong horseshoe magnet, hanging by a thread from the end of a length of garden cane acting as a fishing rod.

Number fishing
This is a very well known game. Little paper fish have small paperclips on their noses and numbers on their sides. The fishpond is a fairly large box or wastepaper basket, placed so that the fish cannot be seen. Fishing rods (of garden cane and thread) are used by each child in turn; and the catch per person is added up, either as a running total, or at the end of a day's fishing.

Flying paperclip
Fix a small strong magnet about 30 cm above the table top, facing (business ends) downwards. An easy way is to put a thin cane through the horseshoe and rest both ends of the cane on piles of books. Tie a length of cotton (choose your colour) to one end of a wire paperclip, let the clip attach itself to the magnet, and then pull it down gently until it is just NOT touching the magnet but still near enough to be attracted. Fix the other end of the cotton down to the table with Plasticine, Blutak, or a small non-metal weight. Try passing paper, plastic, and thin foil through the space between the magnet and the paperclip.

Drawing pin Slalom
(or obstacle race). Make several holes larger than a drawing pin head in rows in a piece of fairly stiff card. Mark IN on one side and OUT on the other. Fix the card flat and firmly between two piles of books so there is room for a hand with a magnet underneath. Put a drawing pin point upwards at IN, and move it between the holes in a weaving route (marked in advance) from IN to OUT without letting it fall through any hole. This can be made easy or difficult. Like the other magnet games, it can be used as a sideshow on Open Days.

Magnetic sorting—back to work

So far all the materials we have tested have been attracted by a magnet. Now collect all sorts of small objects—chalk, rubber, brass, aluminium, copper, wood, foil, silver-coloured plastic or sealing-wax, small stones etc, and mix them up with the nails, hairgrips, washers and paperclips from the earlier experiments. First guess which ones will be attracted by a magnet, then test.

This magnetic sorting is a very good experience, but has a few snags. The main one is that because iron and steel (the magnetic metals) tend to rust, they are often coated thinly with paint or tin or brass. Hence things which look like solid brass (some drawing pins, for example) or are called 'tin' (eg tins) are attracted by a magnet because they are made of iron or steel inside. You need to explain this to children, or to guide them 'to discover' it by scratching off some of the outer layer (brass, paint or tin) and perhaps even letting the iron or steel so uncovered go rusty in shallow water.

NB 1 Many modern 'cans' of the ring-pull opening type are made of aluminium and so are non-magnetic anyway.
NB 2 The trade name Alnico given to some of the strongest magnets suggests that they are made of aluminium, nickel and cobalt. In fact, these magnets have some of each of these metals in them, but they are still more than half iron/steel which is not mentioned in the name.

Bar magnets

Straight magnetized bars of steel (bar magnets) may be brought into the classroom by children; in any case the school should provide them. They show many facts and have important uses which the horseshoe type cannot. Short strong Alnico magnets are excellent, but expensive. With careful treatment they last a very long time, and if they are used to make other small 'play' magnets (see below) the losses into pockets are much reduced.

Bar magnet experiments
1 Test each end against classroom objects, paperclips and non-magnetic materials as in 1 to 7 suggested for horseshoe magnets. This makes it clear that magnets are much the same even if the shape is different—but this shouldn't be taken for granted.

2 Try to pick up as many small paperclips (or panel pins) as possible with one magnet, using the whole length of the bar. This shows up the difference between the ends, which attract strongly, and the middle which hardly picks up anything. Good. Now for a quick think—why is

down, if you have three or more in a string?

4 Make single strings of paperclips hanging from the ends of different magnets. This gives a simple way to compare their strengths. How many clips will hang on?

5 The first paperclip is strongly attracted to the magnet. How strongly is the second, the third, the fourth clip held on? Perhaps the fourth will not even stay attached to the third one. What does this seem to say—that magnetic attraction gets less the further you go away from the magnet?

6 This is an experiment which needs a steady hand. Make a string of say three paperclips hanging from the end of a bar magnet. Take hold of the top paperclip with one finger and thumb, and very gently move the magnet a little way away from it—upwards or sideways (remember the flying paperclip?). Does the chain hang together? Maybe magnetic attraction works at a distance here too. Now take the magnet right away; with even the smallest shake the chain falls to bits. Will a paperclip from the remains pick up another? Perhaps it will just move it, but the main strength was induced (or persuaded) by the bar magnet.

Making magnets

It is too disappointing to try to make good magnets out of paperclips or pieces of 'tin', because they are made of soft iron, and soft iron does not hold magnetism well enough. Steel is the material for permanent magnets; good sources are hairgrips, old nail files, steel (not brass) screws, and if you can still find any, steel knitting needles. Hold the hairgrip, file or other piece of steel in one hand and stroke it from end to end, one way only (like stroking a cat), with one end of your strong bar magnet. Do this several times. Then test the bit of steel by touching a small paperclip, panel pin or drawing pin with it. Other sources of steel which make good magnets, are old hacksaw blades, pieces of old clockspring, and short lengths of curtain net ('giraffe') spring. All of these have the severe disadvantage of sharp edges or ends, and are *not* suitable for young children. Nails, though they look promising, are soft iron and are useless. *NB* For the sake of children's understanding and grasp

a horseshoe magnet so good at picking things up? Maybe because it has two ends side by side? But what about the curved part of the horseshoe—does that behave like the middle of the straight bar? Try it; there is no picking-up strength there either. So horseshoe magnets are simply bar magnets bent into a curve, but straight magnets let us deal with the two ends separately. That's important.

3 Dip one end of a bar magnet into a pile or saucer of paperclips, lift it a little way, and look carefully. Two observations are likely: (*i*) the paperclips don't all hang straight down—some stick out sideways (leave this to be explained some years later); (*ii*) some paperclips are not hanging on the magnet itself, but on other paperclips. This is really interesting. What does it say about the paperclip next to the magnet? Mustn't it mean that the first paperclip is a magnet too? And the second one

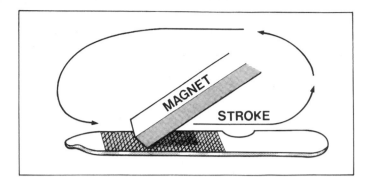

of the ideas of magnetism, stick to simple magnets, and leave electromagnets until years later. Almost all books for children such as Ladybird, and for teachers Science 5/13, follow the A-level textbook habit of putting together electricity and magnetism. But the connection between magnets and electric current is highly complex, and to show children similar results from two such different causes at the same time, can only make science seem incomprehensible. Use simple steel magnets to establish the basic behaviour of a magnet. The going is difficult enough later on; let us grasp one thing at a time, and grasp it thoroughly. It will help later, and will be much more enjoyable.

Two bar magnets

1 Feel the strong attraction between one end (pole) of one bar magnet and one of the poles of its twin, each of them pulling on the other. This gives the clue to the way they should always be put away—side by side and attracting one another. Better still, separate them slightly with a strip of wood or thick card, and add a small piece of soft iron (say a short nail) across each pair of poles, connecting them up.

2 Now turn one magnet round—most children will have done this as part of the magnet fun—and feel the completely different effect as each magnet pushes the other one away. This force of repulsion gives children a great deal of pleasure—there is no visible cause, but an undoubted effect as the two magnets resist and 'try to escape' from touching one another.

3 Use repulsion as the test for two magnets together eg a manufactured magnet and a just-magnetized hairgrip or nail file. Think about this: a bought magnet will attract any piece of iron or steel, so that doesn't tell us anything new about the hairgrip or file, but if one pushes the other away, they must both be magnets. This is important. Children can see as well as feel the effect; for example, a magnetized hairgrip or nail file can be lightly stuck on top of a small raft made from a scrap of expanded polystyrene ceiling tile. Float the raft in a shallow bowl or small tray of water. Pushing the boat can be as effective as pulling it. Fixing the 'home-made' magnet to the raft is necessary, since the strong magnet above the water surface tends just to lift the metal off the raft.

Straight magnets as compasses

The floating magnet left to itself is a compass. Many children know in words that 'a compass needle points North', but few of them have any practical experience of this extraordinary phenomenon. How can we try to give them 'guided discoveries' to see for themselves?

1 Float a strong bar magnet across a raft of ceiling tile or balsa and let it find its own direction. *NB* Keep it in the middle, or surface tension may anchor it to the edge; make sure there are no pieces of iron near the magnet, or its attraction for them may pull it towards them—the one which can move will do so, whichever the attracting object.

2 Fold a strip of paper round the middle of the bar magnet so that it balances horizontally when held up by the ends of the strip. Thread fine cotton (or a long hair if available) through holes in the ends of the paper strip, and hang the magnet up where it can turn freely, away from iron or draught. The advantage of a hair is that it does not unwind itself as some kinds of cotton do when stretched.

3 Magnetize a hairgrip or nail file (etc) and balance it across the top of a thimble or the back of the receiving half of a press-stud. A minute scrap of Plasticine helps. Then push a pin through another piece of ceiling tile

until the head has sunk in, turn the 'stand' point-end upwards, and balance your thimble or press-stud-half on the pin point. This makes a very sensitive compass, which can also be used to test unknown bits of iron or steel for magnetization (by repulsion, not attraction, of course).

Compasses

Some children may own compasses, and the school may also have one or more. These are expensive items, and real care is needed in their use. The two main precautions are (*i*) don't drop them (or they may come off their bearings), and (*ii*) don't 'tease' them with other magnets, especially with strong ones (or their direction may be badly upset—in fact, they may well point to the South instead of to the North). Pupils today sometimes have orienteering experience, perhaps gained with their parents on holidays, and this can be used to the full. They can also be reminded of the unfortunate orienteerer who set his course while still standing in the car park, surrounded by large quantities of iron. If the authorities agree, compass bearings can be marked out on the playground (away from cars) and checked with the plans of the school.

Recording

How are all these experiences with magnets to be recorded by the pupils? It would be worthwhile to keep them together, if at all possible, say in a special 'magnet file' or book, since they are so valuable for work in later years. Probably sketches with a few words here and there will most clearly remind the child of what was done and experienced, and what was learnt. Extensions can well include uses of magnets in everyday life: shutting the doors of fridges and laundrette driers, holding letters on notice boards and paperclips in desk gadgets. Magnetized screwdrivers are used to convey small screws into difficult corners, and needleworkers often have magnetic scissors to pick up dropped pins. There is plenty of scope for the interested child to go further.

Summary suggestions

What knowledge do we expect children to get out of this series of experiments, in addition to the fun?

1 That magnets make something happen (very important to children) and that people (ie the children themselves) can control, and to some extent predict and check, what will happen (which is also important).

2 That the ends (poles) of a magnet, whether straight or curved, attract iron and steel.

3 That many materials, including some metals such as aluminium, are not attracted by a magnet.

4 That magnetic attraction works through 'space' (ie air) and through paper etc.

5 That some metal (actually the soft iron as used in wire paperclips) acts like a magnet as long as there is a magnet very near it, but not otherwise. (This idea is valuable because of its relevance to electromagnets later.)

6 That magnets can be made by stroking steel with the end of a ready-made magnet.

7 That the two ends (poles) of a magnet are different, in that one end of one magnet attracts one end of a second magnet, but the other end of the first magnet pushes it away (repels it).

8 That this pushing-away action only happens when two magnets meet one way round, ie 'head-on'.

9 That this is a test for 'two magnets meeting' since if there is only one magnet the action will be attraction (or nothing).

10 That a lone magnet, away from iron, and able to move, is a compass 'needle', and will point North (and therefore also South). *NB* The end which points to the North, often coloured blue or marked N, is best called the 'North-pointing' pole. This is the easiest way to help children to avoid later difficulties in understanding what really happens.

14 Classroom resources for learning

Each shelf, drawer, cupboard, pinboard, pegboard, bookcase, radiator top or window may provide classroom resources for learning science, as it does for other subject areas. In this chapter we suggest a few possibilities; you will certainly have others, but you may find new ones here.

1 Books

These are the universal resources for learning. Do you have the science books with you in the classroom, or are they concentrated in the school library? Either has its advantages—you have your own preference. Books with many accurate illustrations, such as the *Clue Book* series (Oxford), and *Collins Pocket Guides* are very valuable for identifying 'finds', and obviously this has to be done as soon as possible with live or recently living specimens. And it's a good thing to have a few 'interest' books really handy, maybe some of the best Ladybirds, say *Musical Instruments, Farm Machinery, Prehistoric Animals* and *Aircraft*. If you can afford it, the *AA Book of the British Countryside* is a grand source of information. For ideas on things to do, see some of the best Macdonald Starters: *Look at Walls, Folding and Unfolding* and *Balancing Things,* for example. *The Guinness Book of Records* has a place of its own as a multipurpose item; try it on the boy who always finishes first and then wriggles. 'Find out which is the heaviest land mammal and the lightest land mammal; add their weights together and divide by two to get the median; then see where you come in between them?' Provided he can read, you've kept him occupied. One thing leads to another in that book, even if it is an old edition. Some of the popular books about things to do, such as the *Know How* series eg *Paper Fun,* or Batsford's *Introducing Batik* combine a good deal of science with other activities of classroom value. Why

not make a curtain for the junk corner while learning about wax and water not mixing? They can see examples in Teaching Primary Science *Paints and materials.* Although these books are written for teachers, pupils in Middle Schools have been using and enjoying them in a recent experiment. They looked at the photographs for ideas, consulted the diagrams for instructions, skipped all the bits of educational theory, and worked up some excited discussions over what other children had said, agreeing with or refuting their explanations, and trying out their experiments. The special stimulus was to find children like themselves doing things 'in a book'.

2 The picture library

This is one of the most valuable assets a teacher and a classroom can have. Postcards of animals (not only from the zoo, but from ordinary card shops), of fossils, fish, frogs etc from the Natural History Museum; of aircraft and ships from the Science Museum; of harps and harpsichord from the Victoria and Albert Museum. Add a few at every opportunity. Travel brochures provide superb 'blue sky pictures' to illustrate 'horizontal' with distant horizons; the Sunday supplements sometimes have a useful picture, the BBC handbooks of previous years are excellent, and even breakfast cereals may contribute usefully. Once you start collecting material for such an enterprise you find that it is an indispensable aid. Next time a child asks which way the stripes go on a zebra you don't need to say 'up and down on the body, round and round on the legs'—he or she can find out.

Another important 'looking-up' function of the same picture library is the extension of children's individual vocabularies. A picture with a word (perhaps on the back) helps the child who either doesn't know, or doesn't know it in English, but who may not want to ask. Looking things up in the picture library is a very respectable way to find out things.

Organization   If they are to be successful, pictures must be protected. The hazards of fingers, floor, and the temptation of ball-point additions, mean that any picture worth keeping is worth protecting. Plastic film and a backing card will be the most common method. The best method is more expensive, but takes much less of the teacher's scarce resources of time and energy. This is to put the picture into a transparent plastic pocket, open only at one end. These are supplied by some authorities for cookery recipes, and are sold commercially to cover job cards; some are in A4 size only, which is extravagant, since most pictures for individual children's use are or can be postcard-sized. A 20 x 12.5 cm (8 x 5 inch) size is very convenient, or an A5 format if the makers are up to date. Apart from the convenience of speed in covering material in this way, there is the saving in cash, once covers have been bought, in that sets can be transferred out of and into covers for special topics. This week it may be 'mother-and-baby animal' pictures (a very popular one, to which the class will contribute too), and next week it will be 'wheels everywhere', and so on.

The other main factor in efficient use of resource material is, of course, retrieval. You must be able to find what you want when you want it, often in a hurry. Again, the best way costs more, though it is adaptable and long lasting. This is to put the pictures in their protective covers into transparent polystyrene food containers (which can double as small size aquaria or cages for snails etc when occasion demands). Stewart Plastics, of Purley Way, Croydon make them in very high quality, and stackable, which helps. If funds only allow for shoeboxes, then good labelling is of the first importance —preferably on top, side and end, so that no matter how it gets stacked, the box can be found at once.

3 Slide viewer

Many people have a small slide viewer for holiday transparencies—not a projector, just a small daylight or battery-powered device. This makes a fine extension to the classroom picture library, and can be used by individual children. It is not expensive and most kinds are tough. Transparencies are everywhere, though specifically scientific ones have to be looked for. The Geological Museum in London has some superb ones of crystals, rocks and caves, while many visitors to the zoo take their own, and may have more than they need afterwards. These can be of great use to children who can't remember just how the giraffe's horns grow, or how long the gibbon's tail is (if it has one). Slide viewers need not only be for casual 'entertainment'; with a worksheet a pupil or two can make notes, answer questions, make sketches and even invent a quiz for others (a popular job) using one or two slides. Beyond the facts they pick up (the jigsaw shapes of the giraffe's spots, the camouflage light-coloured underside compensating for shadow in bright sunlight) children learn to enjoy concentrating their attention, and begin to see details which would never have been noticed otherwise.

Storage   Transparencies need more careful handling and storage than postcards, of course. There are useful wallets for the job, but children need to learn beforehand only to handle them by the frames.

Classification is a question for each teacher to think about. Are you going to use the library decimal classes from the beginning, as they do in the children's sections of public libraries? This numbering means nothing to children, but at least if they get used to it, they will be able to find the science books they want to look at in the adult library. And slides can have the same classification as books.

4 What else, besides books and pictures?

There are some resources which are so often useful in the classroom that once you and the class become used to them, you all wonder how anybody else manages without. One such resource is the large magnifying glass, or more than one if you can manage it. The big Osmiroid Magnispector, made of plastic, is fine; they sell it with a box to hold the minibeasts, but this box has a most distracting millimetre grid in the bottom. The thing to do is to buy the lens on a plain box, if possible, and if you need millimetre squares in it, drop in a piece of squared paper.

5 The classroom clock

This is an important item for many pieces of scientific observation, as well as being useful when activities are going to need some clearing up time. Since children of all ages have an elastic time sense ('only another minute') the best way to help them to understand the passage of time is to show them a clock with a sweep-hand going round once a minute. No other movement of clock hands is fast enough for them to take it in. If this is possible, try it. Many of the simple wall clocks (such as those made by Smith's and kept in time by a tiny tuning fork inside (which you can only hear if you put your ear to the back of the clock) are powered by a single-cell dry battery (eg HP 11, 1.5 volts). This lasts for over a year, and doesn't suffer from power cuts.

6 Bits for battery circuits

The young and the young at heart enjoy making small electric light bulbs light up. The only way to make sure that every pupil in a class gets an adequate chance to experience this fun is to have the materials available in the classroom, not stored away in a 'science cupboard' elsewhere.

What do we need as a minimum collection of resources? At rock bottom all we need is a few 2.5-volt torch bulbs, some copper wire and one or two 3-volt batteries. The bulbs can be bought at Woolworths, though if a school buys them in any quantity a very good source (efficient, quick and inexpensive) is R. S. Components Ltd., 13, Epworth Street, E.C.2. The batteries, as used in bicycle lamps, need to be bought just before use; their shelf-life is quite long, but it is a pity to waste any of it.

As for the wire, a most satisfactory kind for classroom battery circuits is the kind the telephone engineers sometimes scatter in short lengths when they have just finished a re-wiring job. This particular wire has advantages apart from its being free. It is thin enough to be bent easily without pliers, it is insulated by a layer or 'sleeving' of plastic (except for the ends, which one

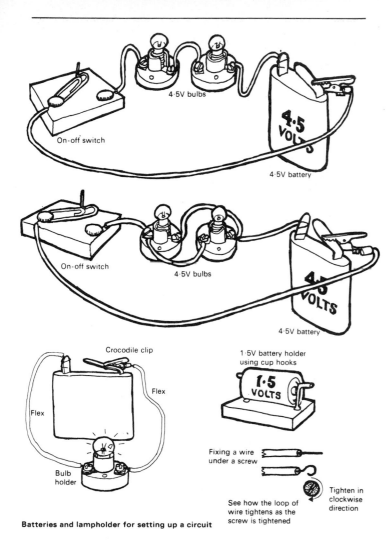

4·5V bulbs

On-off switch

4·5V battery

On-off switch

4·5V bulbs

4·5V battery

Crocodile clip

Flex

Flex

Bulb holder

1·5V battery holder using cup hooks

1·5 VOLTS

Fixing a wire under a screw

See how the loop of wire tightens as the screw is tightened

Tighten in clockwise direction

Batteries and lampholder for setting up a circuit

Minimum circuits can be built up with just the three items, battery, bulb and wires. For classroom uses this will sometimes be enough, eg to put a light in the dolls' house or inside the paste jar on top of the bleach bottle lighthouse. The wire can be twisted round the contact strips on the battery, and round the screw contact at the base of the bulb, with the little lead knob under the bulb resting in a small loop of wire to make the second contact. But what else do we need, to have an adequate experimental kit, or perhaps to fit up a puppet theatre in the classroom with internal lighting? The main further items will be bulb holders (sometimes called batten holders in catalogues) into which the bulbs are screwed for better contact, some small blocks of wood sawn from a length of batten, and two items from the school office: a few drawing pins and some large wire paperclips.

Excellent illustrations showing circuits, switches, lay-out boards and varied experimental work using this simple apparatus are found in a form usable by children themselves in such books as *Nuffield Junior Science Apparatus* (Collins, 1967), Science 5/13 *Early*

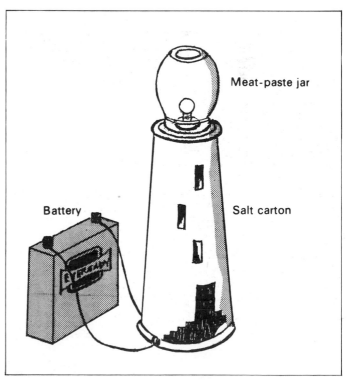

Meat-paste jar

Battery

Salt carton

has to uncover anyway to make a contact) and the plastic is, if one is lucky, in a number of attractive colours. People who do physics in laboratories often seem to think that wire for electric circuits must be covered in red or black plastic; for good reasons of their own (ie to match up our telephone lines again) the Post Office has different ideas. Children should know that so long as there is copper wire inside it, the plastic insulation can be peach-coloured or pale blue—and this small thing can make 'electricity' seem a more approachable science.

experiences (Schools Council/Macdonald Educational, 1972) and *Science from toys* (Schools Council/ Macdonald Educational, 1972).

The scope for inventive children using this perfectly safe electrical apparatus is enormous. The one condition which any responsible teacher will make from the very beginning is that *only* battery-powered low-voltage circuits may be experimented with; *no* mains current.

---

7 Wooden clothes pegs

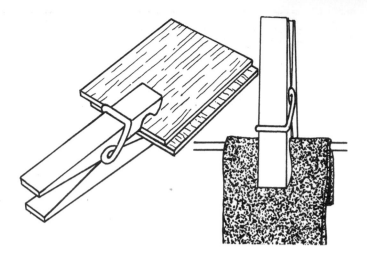

One of the most ingenious torch bulb holders invented by a school pupil and shown in Nuffield Junior Science Apparatus uses an ordinary spring wooden clothes peg to hold the bulb and the wire-ends in correct contact. There are many variations on this, eg using a drawing pin inside each of the 'jaws' of the peg as contacts, and working the peg to signal in Morse code with a light bulb. Buzzers are rather a nuisance in the classroom. Another variation, invented by a child, is to hold a soluble aspirin tablet in the peg so that if the peg is left on the windowsill, rain will dissolve the tablet and allow the peg to close, thus making a bell ring, signalling that the washing should be brought in.

Clothes pegs are in other ways very handy in the class-room: they hold fabric-printing or large tie-and-dye cloths up out of the way until dry; they hold test squares of D.I.Y. plywood (see *Science from wood*)

until the glue has stuck the matchbox layers together; they support paper screens for shadow experiments; and they can be used for holding hot tin lids. With a thin string through the spring a clothes peg will hold up a plastic bag, say of collected leaves, until needed. A row of pegs strung on a string holds up a whole curtain until the batik is dry.

What do we want our pupils to gain in the classroom? A wide range of interesting experiences, all sorts of helpful skills, some factual knowledge, lively minds, and in particular the ability and confidence to cope with whatever they meet. Many small factors go into this attitude; the more we can provide, the better.

15 Solving practical problems

The early stages of being a scientist involve seeing what happens—learning about real materials *from* the materials, *not* from books or people. Of course these are important too, but hearing or reading about the theory of levers is pointless if you've never used a lever, or if you don't know you've used one. The old academic teaching method of 'here's the Law; now let's make a list of its uses', for example—crowbar . . . 'Miss, what's a crowbar?' 'No idea, Pat. I don't think I've ever seen one,' gives no confidence for dealing with the next problem. Practical experiences teach people how to cope, and even if the exact method is not transferable, the confidence is.

Children need their experiences to be concrete, and the younger the child, the more concrete the experience should be. They progress from techniques to simple technology, which may later be followed by the intellectual 'click'—'Oh, so that's how it happens, that's why it happens', the 'ah-ha' phenomenon of comprehension and explanation.

Guided discovery is essential. Life is too short and time too precious for any child to have to find out everything from scratch. But we can help children to ask 'If we do this, what is likely to happen?' followed by 'Does it happen?', and then as the next step 'If we want this to happen, what can we do which might make it happen?' followed by 'Does it work?' Such logical thinking and testing is as important in political and economic life as in science.

Science 5/13 With objectives in mind suggests for 'infants generally' Objective 1.41 *Ability to find answers to simple problems by investigation;* and for Stage 2, (concrete operations, later stage, 'not merely 9-11-year-olds') Objectives 2, 11 and 2.41 *Enjoyment in developing methods for solving problems or testing ideas* and *Ability to frame questions likely to be answered through investigations.*

In all the Teaching Primary Science texts there are suggestions for ways to achieve these ends. Here are some more starting points.

1 A picture which isn't real, or 'the image on the wall'

This is an extraordinary effect, never questioned by millions of cinema goers, film-strip viewers and takers of holiday slides. Switch off the projector, and the picture isn't there any more. What is more embarrassing than putting the slide into the projector so that you see everything right way up as you put it in and it then comes out upside down on the screen or wall? Writing or street signs may be backwards as well; everybody notices things like that. Don't tell children what they ought to have done; it's too late. Help them to turn the whole thing into a successful piece of scientific research. Try it once again to make sure, then turn the transparency round, or upside down, or over, only one move at a time, and look again at the screen. Only changing one thing at a time is a very important piece of scientific method; understanding its importance comes to children late, but you can suggest it in passing, and the hint will be comprehended later. It is better than the frenzied 'change everything all at the same time' performance of unscientific characters, and makes children feel as if they are in control of events—as in fact they are if they do it this step-by-step way. Then take it further, by guiding them to check the result when they have found 'the right way round and up' for one slide. Does it work, as we asked before, for other slides? Try several; good scientists are only happy with a result if it works over and over again. Ask another child or better a small group of children to try it, and then discuss their results with the first experimenter(s).

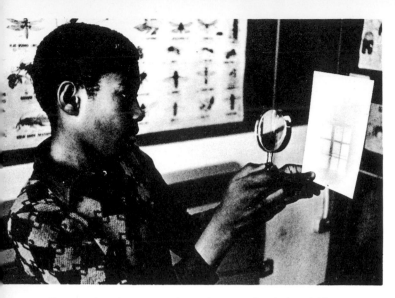

that it was there; the others saw it too, and it's now in the book. When the children go round the school with magnifying glasses showing off this result, they're 'hooked'. Test it in another way, using a candle flame instead of a transparency or a window—see Teaching Primary Science *Candles*, p. 31. A temporary screen to keep the sunlight away from the image helps to make it easier to see. The traditional 'pinhole camera', made from a tin can with a small hole in the middle of the bottom and greaseproof paper over the open end, shows that you don't even need a magnifying glass; the hole will do instead of the lens. This time the screening is best done by rolling a folded newspaper round the greaseproof paper end of the tin, so that it sticks out. Then look along the paper tube to see the image of the candle flame on the greaseproof paper 'screen'. In *Candles* there is a teacher trying it, in the photograph on page 33. Pupils who know about using astronomical telescopes will also know that with the ordinary kind of telescope they see the moon 'upside down'; this does not matter too much. Children lucky enough to be using microscopes will have found that when they push the object on the slide from left to right, they see the thing going from right to left—and the same 'opposite effect' happens when they move the slide towards themselves—the object seems to move away (ie the image moves the opposite way). For younger children who see them such events can be left as experiences, things which happen. Older or more able pupils may begin to generalize about rays of light going through the pinhole (from the top of the candle flame to the bottom of the image) and will find good lens diagrams in books about light, eg Nuffield Physics Classroom Guide *Optical Instruments* by G. W. Dorling (Longman/Penguin, 1969).

For a scientist a sound result or method should be reproducible; there is always doubt about the bent spoon or the 'ectoplasm' which only one person can produce.

Next take it a step further, and look with the pupils for at least a partial explanation, but again on a practical basis. The boy in the photograph did not expect what he got on his sheet of paper, but there was no doubt

2 How to make a balance balance

A very important part of children's early science and mathematics is the experience of balancing equal masses, using an equal-armed balance. Good apparatus for this is the Osmiroid new Super Beamer or ESA Primary Balance (with either plastic pans or buckets). Frequently after use with water, sand etc the two pans do not balance exactly. If they happen to balance

perfectly, one can always manage, as if by accident, to make sure that there is a little piece of Plasticine stuck under one pan so that the beam is definitely not level. Many younger children will not notice this at all, or if they do, will not think it matters. However, if we now start the innocent game with plenty of plastic one-gram 'weights' (such as Invicta stackable blue ones, or E. J. Arnold's small red ones) of 'you put one in your pan, Peter puts one in his pan' (both using the same make to keep it 'fair'), the advantage should be seen to be on one side all the time. The children will be observing the balance by now, because each has a personal interest in the equality of the two sides. Well, why not change ends? That's what they do in football matches, to make it fair. And the 'advantage' is seen to go with one of the balance pans . . . 'that one is always heavier than this one'.

Good. What next? There are two easy alternatives, which may well be suggested by the two children involved. (a) find out what makes one side heavier than the other, or (b) simply make the lighter side a bit heavier (with a piece of Plasticine). With a little encouragement both children can see both alternatives; this is scientific thinking too. One of them can find the original bit of Plasticine; each can look at and test the sliding adjustment which the makers have built in for just this unbalanced condition (called a compensator or zero adjuster). The pupils may want to try the effect of moving this sliding adjuster to the extreme ends of its range, first one way, then the other. If they propose this, they are showing exactly the scientific inquisitiveness we welcome. In addition, they have collected an experience of the principle of moments—which in non-mathematical terms they can probably grasp quite readily—the further you sit from the middle of the seesaw, the heavier you seem to be. A small child right at the end of the seesaw can balance a much heavier one sitting near the middle. If the heaviest child sits at the very end, you have to organize your friends on to the other end.

But the next time these children come to use the balance they are likely (a) to look and see if it balances before they begin, and (b) to know what to do if it doesn't—in other words, they know how to cope, and are confident in their control of the balance situation.

3 Learning to be inventive

Inventions which work are one of the greatest assets any country can produce. Let us help our pupils to investigate materials, to test ideas, and to think out effective ways of putting them together into inventions for solving problems. Edward de Bono showed in his 'dog-exercising' book that children have plenty of ideas—but testing with real apparatus is the next essential step.

Making a mirror stand up on the classroom table can become a child-sized challenge, with excellent results. Just give them the mirrors, plastic ones preferably, and the sort of oddments shown in the book *Mirrors and magnifiers* page 5. One child used two ordinary wooden clothes pegs, one at each bottom corner of the mirror; it worked perfectly. Others tried Plasticine; this holds the mirror, but it makes a greasy mark on the paper underneath, and another on the mirror. When you have several contributions, why not ask for votes or a 'best buy' estimate from other pupils. Then show them any of the ideas illustrated which they have not yet thought of. If they need to see the mirror image at the bottom edge of the mirror some of these are useless.

What do we want our pupils to gain and keep for life out of their science work in the primary years? Perhaps the most important general idea and the most valuable to their society as well as to themselves, is that problems *are* soluble, and that ways of solving them *are* available.

We shall hope that the children will have sufficient basic experiences and confidences to be:

problem-seeing; problem-seeking; problem attacking; and problem-solving.

Such achievement will demand ideas, creativity and 'know-how'. Ideas, such as the age-old dream of perpetual motion, come to people with lively minds; but the second essential must follow: this idea—does it work? And for many good ideas, which after testing are found to work, one can say 'it's easy when you know how'.

Index